P9-ASB-610

WITHDRAWN

FINDING OUT ABOUT THE EARLY RUSSIANS

Other titles in this series:

Finding Out About Ancient Egypt
by H. E. L. Mellersh

Finding Out About the Incas
by C. A. Burland

Finding Out About the EARLY RUSSIANS

Tamara Talbot Rice

Introduction by

Harrison E. Salisbury

Lothrop, Lee & Shepard, New York

First American edition 1964

Library of Congress Catalog Card Number: 64-14442

The majority of the photographs in the book are from the personal collection of the author, but we are also grateful to the Picture Collection of the New York Public Library, the Victoria and Albert Museum, and the British Society for Cultural Relations with the U.S.S.R. for their help in supplying us with additional photographs.

The line drawings are by Margaret Scott.

The maps are by Ursula Suess.

Table of Contents

List of Illustrations

Introduction

by Harrison E. Salisbury

THE HISTORY of any country and its culture is a skein of many strands and many colors, inextricably mixed. That of Russia is no exception. Indeed, located as she is on the broad open land mass of Europe and Asia, the Russian nation has been subjected to an incredible mixture of influences—the nomadic wanderings of the Scyths and Sarmatians, the devastation of the Huns of East Asia, the evangelical missions of the Greek Orthodox Church, the half-trade, half-warrior incursions of the Vikings, the conquests of German knights and Polish barons, the sea commerce of the English and the Dutch, the art of France and Italy, the science and philosophy of Germany.

And those are only a handful of the scores of currents, crosscurrents, invasions and conquests, influences and counterinfluences, which have worked to give shape and content to the nation we know today as Russia.

America and the United States is such a late-comer to the world scene that we know almost every item of its history. But Russia is so ancient that even the name of the country is a mystery over which historians endlessly quarrel, some insisting that it came in with the Vikings or Varangers. Others find its derivation in the name for a tribe of Alans, a long-vanished people from Persia.

These may seem like musty questions for the historic archives. They are not. Within them lies the key to that enigma, wrapped in riddle, shrouded in mystery, which is what Winston Churchill called Russia. If we know who the Russians are, whence they came, and the history of their trials and tribulations, we can more easily understand what they are today and, at least in part, why they constitute a problem in the world.

For instance, the great Russian historian Klyuchevsky believed that the most important single fact about Russia was its location on a vast sealike plain, open to invasion from east, from west, from north, from south. Unlike other countries Russia had few natural frontiers. The Urals are a low mountain range, no barrier to any army. The great mountain ranges of Asia are easily bypassed along grassy plateaus and flat deserts. To the north and northeast there is only mile after mile of forest, and in the west the biggest obstacles are trackless marshes.

Thus, in every epoch Russia has been invaded. Her people have come to equate the foreigner with the invader, to look toward the horizon not with confidence but fear. Out of this has grown a national tendency toward hostility and suspicion to those beyond the border which, even today, complicates Russia's relations with other nations.

Also it has made Russia a melting pot. The United

States is a congeries of peoples because immigrants from so many lands made their way here to seek a new home and fortune. Russia is a great mixture of peoples because of the many invasions which have left remnants and marks. And, in addition, Russia is a vigorous nation which has expanded rapidly in every direction from its original stronghold around ancient Kiev and the principality of Muscovy.

In Czarist days Russia was known as the "prison house of nations" because so many different peoples were held subject to the Imperial throne. With the coming of Communism most of those peoples have been retained and incorporated within what is known now as the Union of Soviet Socialist Republics. There are fifteen of these so-called Republics. By far the largest is the Russian Republic, which includes all of European Russia and Siberia. In all there are some one hundred and eighty-five distinguishable peoples in the Soviet Union, each with its own national customs, language, and history. The Soviet fabric, as can be seen, is a diverse and colorful one.

When we read of the early history of the nation which was to become Russia we encounter one unfamiliar name after another—the names of peoples who have long since disappeared and who seem to have vanished with hardly a trace—the Scythians, the Alans, the Roxalans, the Sarmatians, the Cimmerians, the Huns, the Ossetians, the Avars, the Ugrians, the Khazars, the Polovtsians.

But each of these peoples has left a recognizable mark somewhere on the history and being of the Russian nation. Some of these strange peoples actually still exist in tiny clusters, often high up in a remote mountain valley of the Caucasus or the Altai mountains in Asia. The Ossetians, for instance, can still be found in the Soviet Republic of Georgia. Others survive only in art and archaeological remains, like the Scyths and the Sarmatians. The Khazars, a fascinating nomad tribe which adopted Judaism, have left their trace in names and customs in the Volga River basin. The Polovtsians are immortalized in a famous dance in Borodin's opera, *Prince Igor.*

Of course these are not the only traces. Nor necessarily the most important. The old saying, "Scratch a Russian, find a Tartar," epitomizes the most important effect upon Russia of centuries of movement of people, both warlike and peaceful, between Asia and Europe. The great nomadic invasions from the East—those of the Scyths, the Sarmatians, the Mongols, the Huns—have left indelible marks on Russian character. Some of these are visible in the physical characteristics of many Russians—high cheekbones and, sometimes, even the more slanted Asiatic eyes.

If we study the Russian language we find that mixed in with the Slavic words (the original Slavs were a peaceful pastoral people living in eastern Europe, largely to the west of present-day Russia) are vast admixtures of words and terms from the various Asian tribes. Indeed, many customs (the ancient peasant full bow, so similar to the Oriental kowtow) clearly derive from

Asia. And some psychological investigators believe that the characteristic slyness and suspicion of the Slav peasants may have come out of the long centuries when they were enthralled by Mongol masters and could survive only by deceit and cleverness.

Even the Russian landscape betrays the mixture of Europe and Asia—the bulbous onion domes of the Orthodox churches with their bright blue and gilt-starred roofs bringing an echo of Constantinople to the vast expanse of birch and pine forest. The influence of Byzantine Greece with its rich imagery, its pomp and pageantry, its ritual and circumstance, is unmistakably preserved even in the great Communist spectacles of Red Square. The procession past the Lenin Mausoleum had its precedent in the triumphal marches of ancient Rome.

But when all this has been said about the East and its influence upon Russia, we constantly must return to the essential European nature of the country. Asia gives Russia color, barbaric hues, vestiges of an Oriental past. But it is Europe which dominates Russia's culture and heritage. Kiev, Russia's ancient capital, was a powerful and advanced European city when London was just a rude town. The Kremlin towers owe their beauty to architects who came from or studied under the great masters of Florence.

After the long Mongol oppression, Russian ruler after ruler struggled to bring his nation back to Europe. None thought of Asia as his primary sphere. Ivan the Terrible,

Peter the Great, Catherine the Great, Alexander I, and even Lenin were Europeans and thought of themselves as Europeans. It was the Europe of Elizabeth of England which Ivan envied. It was the Europe of industrialized Holland and London which Peter sought to imitate. It was the brilliant Europe of the French Encyclopedists which attracted Catherine. It was Great Power Europe of Napoleon and Metternich and the Congress of Vienna which was the sphere of Alexander. And Lenin, leader of the Bolshevik Revolution, found his inspiration in the German social philosophy of Karl Marx and, himself, spent half his adult life in western Europe, reading French, German, and English almost as easily as Russian.

So this is Russia—the Soviet Union of today. A land which straddles Europe and Asia, partaking of the qualities of a myriad of cultures which are blended into a mixture peculiarly and specifically Russian; a land of ancient and diverse roots, a nation of multi-sided people, incredibly varied in appearance, characteristics, and beliefs—the product of its geography and its history.

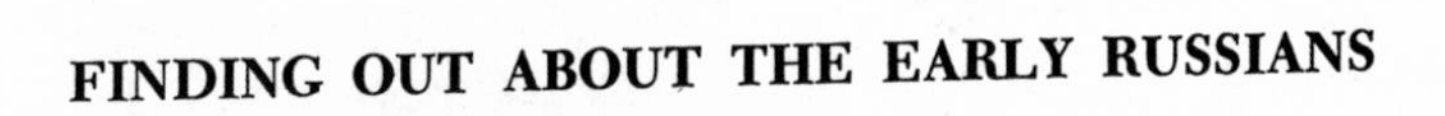

FINDING OUT ABOUT THE EARLY RUSSIANS

Discovering the Russian Past

Most of us love to listen to stories about ourselves when we were small, and many of us are equally fond of listening to stories about our country at a time when it, too, was very young. Indeed there are few people whose imaginations are not stirred by contact with the past.

It is because practically each one of us has within himself a feeling for history that the past interests us, but this interest is inclined to remain unawakened until some outer event brings it to life. In young nations the historical sense is generally aroused by feelings of patriotism, which are themselves the result of political growth; among individuals, interest either in the past or in a foreign country is often awakened by some beautiful object

Peter the Great. Bronze bust by Rastrelli, c. 1725.

or some ancient tale delving into remote ages and unfamiliar civilizations.

In Russia, it was only under Peter the Great (1682–1725) and his successors on the Russian throne that this natural interest in the past was able to take root, to flourish and expand, first into a delight in antiquities, then into a lasting, keen, and scholarly pursuit of history and archaeology.

Peter the Great, Czar, or sovereign, of Russia, did much toward introducing the customs of western Europe into Russia. When still a young man he traveled in western Europe, visiting great palaces filled with splendid works of art of various origins and dates, and he also worked as a shipbuilder both in Holland and in England.

Peter took pains to note all the military, naval, scientific, and industrial achievements of the English, and upon his return to Moscow, which was then as now the capital of Russia, he was determined to make his country as efficient and as up to date as the most advanced European states.

Peter was also anxious to make his people take an interest in their country's past, and to provide Russia with buildings and collections of works of art as splendid as those which he had taken delight in when he visited the great European capitals.

While he was traveling in western Europe he had begun collecting beautiful and curious objects as well as lovely paintings, and in 1703 he decided to build a new town with an outlet to the sea to replace landlocked Moscow as his capital. He chose for it a site on the banks of the river Neva, and called it St. Pieterborck (St. Peter's town) after his patron saint. Abandoning Moscow, he installed himself there, often joining the thousands of workmen toiling in the swampy soil to help them build the new town. It became famous as St. Petersburg, one of Europe's loveliest cities, and is known to us today as Leningrad.

As soon as the essential government offices had been finished, Peter started improving the house which the German architect Schlüter had built for him, carving his own paneling for it, and arranging the objects and pictures which he had bought during his travels abroad. He set many of his Dutch pictures into the paneling of the hall in the enchanting little villa of *Mon Plaisir*, which he reserved for his own use on the shore of the Gulf of Finland. It was in a wooded area some fifteen miles to the west of his new capital, near the spot where his great palace of Peterhof with its magnificent garden of fountains was being built. He also gave orders for a building on the left bank of the Neva in St. Petersburg, which he was to call his Cabinet of Curios, and which became part of the Russian Academy of Sciences. Peter intended to keep his geological and anatomical collections in it, but he soon used it also for the various antiquities which he acquired.

In quite a short time Peter's Cabinet of Curios began to attract considerable attention, largely because of some fine but curious objects in gold, silver, and bronze which were being discovered in various parts of Russia either by peasants who had begun to plough their fields more deeply than their forebears or by people who had started to cultivate what had until then been forest land.

Soon the collection was increased by the activities of enterprising looters who succeeded in tunneling into

A pierced gold buckle of Siberian workmanship from the third to second century B.C. *Shaped in the form of a horizontal letter B, it represents a hunt. From Peter the Great's collection of antiquities, it is now in the Hermitage.*

some of the ancient burial mounds which exist in considerable numbers in Siberia and in the great plain that stretches across the whole of southern Russia and which is known as the Eurasian plain—"Eurasia" being formed by blending the names of Europe and Asia into one word.

In addition to objects found in Russia, Peter also began collecting good examples of early metal work, whether Achaemenid—that is to say, ancient Persian—or Graeco-Bactrian. He was also very fond of Oriental armor and he acquired fine specimens of Turkish, Persian, Italian, and even Indonesian workmanship. All these objects were later to serve as the kernel around which were formed the fantastically rich collections on view today in the Hermitage Museum in Leningrad.

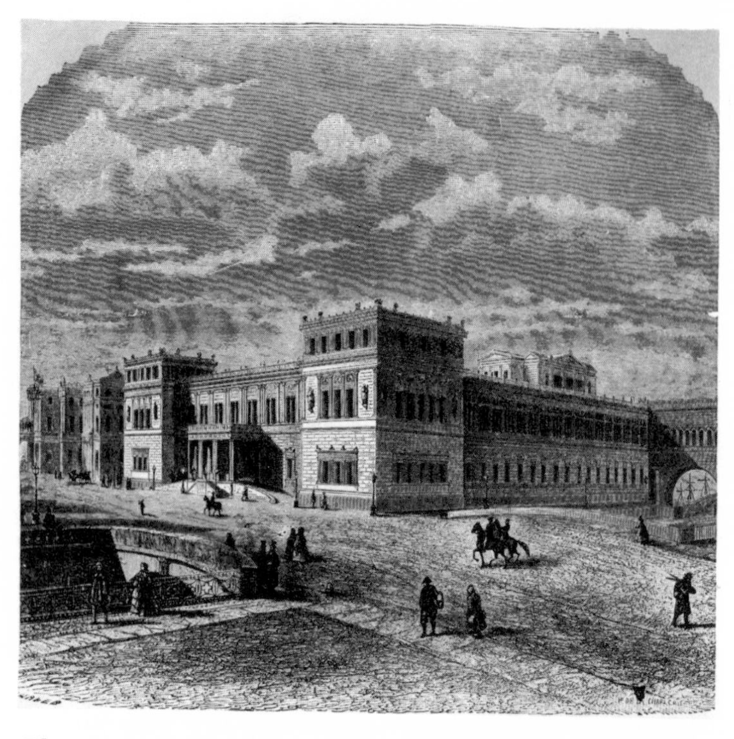

The Hermitage Museum, Leningrad. From a nineteenth century engraving.

Peter's delight in beautiful objects made collecting a fashionable hobby among his courtiers, but they pursued it in a rather magpie-like manner, acquiring objects which appealed to them without pausing to consider them in their archaeological or historical setting—without attempting to learn from each object something about the way of life and the outlook of the people who had been responsible for creating it. It was not until long

Catherine the Great.

after Peter's death, in fact not until the reign of Catherine the Great of Russia (1762–96), that the discovery of Pompeii, and the scientific excavations carried out on that long-buried city, came as a revelation not only to western Europe but also to Russia, suddenly showing the educated Russians the fascination and the value of historical studies.

Carried away by the general enthusiasm, Catherine the Great also began collecting European paintings. Following Peter's example, she likewise set about acquiring Oriental works of art so as to fill some of the gaps Peter had left. She concentrated on Egyptian objects, but she also bought Mesopotamian and Persian antiquities, as well as Byzantine and Chinese ones.

Many well-to-do Russians now became keen and well-informed collectors, and some of the great families of merchant princes—families whose cultural activities can to some extent be compared to those of the Medici of medieval Italy—concentrated on acquiring Russian antiquities. They were encouraged in this by the Russian Academy of Sciences which, though founded by Peter the Great in 1724, greatly extended its scope under Catherine. It is still the institution which, with its modern regional branches, remains responsible for all the archaeological work carried out today in Soviet Russia. The many-sided activities of the Academy also acted as a spur to literary as well as to historical research, and as a result the oldest Russian epic, the lovely twelfth century poem known as *The Lay of Igor's Campaign,* was discovered in one of the state archives in 1775.

Though Catherine did so much to encourage historical and literary studies, and to develop an understanding of great painting, it is surprising to find that the real incentive to archaeological work in Russia was provided by Napoleon—the very man who, in 1812, overran much of western Russia and was responsible for the destruction of Moscow by fire. However, in 1798, any fears of future war between Russia and France were obscured in Russia by the respect which Russians felt for the manner in which Napoleon had embarked on a difficult military campaign in Egypt. The French general had taken with him not only his troops, equipment, and provisions but also a band of scholars and scientists whom he had engaged in order that they might make a survey of Egypt's monuments and antiquities.

The publication of their work prompted Russians to follow Napoleon's lead and examine their native antiquities. Archaeology became with them a recognized science and a rewarding occupation. Numerous archaeological societies sprang up in Russia; and excavations were undertaken which, with the passing years, shed their resemblance to glorified treasure hunts and became serious expeditions. Their number grew throughout the nineteenth century. Chance finds, either of single objects or graves or of great hordes of considerable monetary value as well as of outstanding historical and artistic interest, continued to be made, each adding to our knowledge of the past and also to the array of precious and beautiful objects in Russia's museums.

Since the Revolution of 1917 the number of excavations undertaken in the U.S.S.R., the Union of Soviet Socialist Republics—the name by which post-revolutionary Russia is known—has greatly increased, for the whole of that vast country is immensely rich both in ancient sites and in burial grounds, some of which date as far back as the third millennium B.C., though others are as recent as the ninth century or so A.D.

The excavations which are being carried out today in Russia are conducted with great skill and efficiency.

They have produced a vast amount of new material, some of which, as for example that recovered from the frozen burial mounds of the northern Altai in western Siberia or from Armenia, have revealed the existence of entirely new, wholly unsuspected, immensely fascinating cultures. Furthermore, whereas in the nineteenth century Russian archaeologists were largely concerned with obtaining works of art and in establishing the broad historical outlines of the civilizations which had grown up on Russia's soil at one time or another, modern archaeologists are equally interested in the social and economic conditions which affected the lives of the people living in those periods.

Because of the change in outlook, archaeology has developed into an exact science. As a result, every object, however small and coarsely made, has become as important as the most beautiful and valuable find because it may well be able to throw more light on general conditions of its own day than the supremely lovely object made for a single, often highly privileged person.

The attention with which all finds are examined today has produced a great deal of detailed information. The picture of the past which has emerged is sufficiently complete to enable us to form a fairly clear idea of the way in which the various groups of people lived who succeeded each other from prehistoric times onward in some of the more fertile areas of what is known to us today as Russia.

The Earliest Russians

THE U.S.S.R. is so vast a country that, in antiquity, events which occurred in one part of it did not necessarily affect the rest.

Geographically, the whole of the territory of the U.S.S.R. can be divided into a series of horizontal bands or belts. The northernmost of these, bordering the Arctic Ocean, is known as the tundra belt because of the moss which grows on its vast swamps. In ancient times it was inhabited by Lapp, Samoyed, and Tungus nomads living off reindeer flesh and fish.

Moving southward, the tundra gives way to a forest belt in which much of the woodland has been cut down throughout the centuries. This is in turn succeeded by a narrow strip of parkland, to the south of which stretches the great plain or steppe known as the Eurasian plain because it extends virtually unbroken from present-day Hungary to the borders of China. In its Asiatic section, its fertile grasslands give way in places to barren salt deserts. In western Asia its northern section abuts on the mountains of the Altai.

In ancient times it was far easier for people to obtain the basic foodstuffs essential to life in the Eurasian plain than in the other belts. This was especially true of its European section because numerous rivers flow through it. Some are vast ones such as the Volga, which is the longest river in Europe, and the Don, Dnieper, and Dniester. Others, such as the Bug or the Kama, though smaller, have always been important as waterways. And there are a great many even smaller rivers, all of them rich in fish and also extremely useful as a means of transport.

Because of these advantages the south Russian plain, as the European section of this vast grazing ground is often called, attracted inhabitants from very early times. Many of those who followed each other through the years left their mark in the form of the mounds which they raised above the burials of their dead. Burial is the word archaeologists use for an ancient grave or tomb.

The number of these mounds is very considerable; they vary not only in date but also in their shapes and sizes. Some of the largest and most interesting have been found in southern Russia, mainly in the basins of the rivers Don and Dnieper, in the Crimea, and in the strip

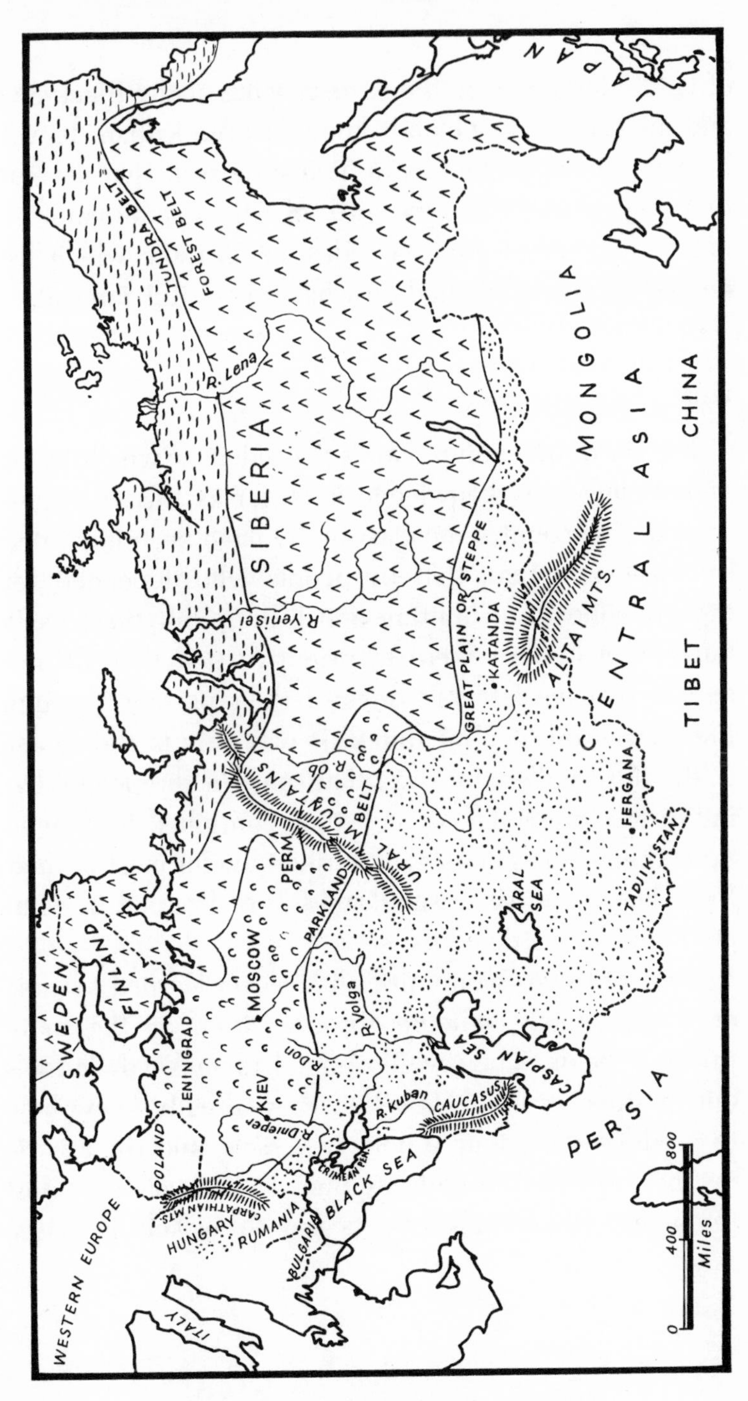

Geographical map of Russia (the U.S.S.R.)

of land lying between the eastern shore of the Black Sea and the Caucasus, which is known as the Kuban. It was in these areas, as well as in Transcaucasia, that several thousand years before the birth of Christ small communities of people created the oldest civilizations which are known to have flourished on what is now Russian soil.

Hunters and Fishers

The third millennium B.C. is the oldest of which we at present have any knowledge in so far as Russia is concerned. The country must assuredly have been inhabited for far longer than that by people who depended for their livelihood on hunting and fishing, but these early families of hunters were so primitive that they do not appear to have left any trace of their passage through life on the soil they inhabited. It was only in the course of the third millennium B.C. that some of the people living in the forest belt, though they continued to depend upon their skill as hunters and fishermen for most of their food, began to live in small mud huts grouped in what are known as settlements.

None of these communities had as yet learned to mine or shape metals, whether bronze, iron, or the more precious kinds. They were obliged to make their tools out of stone or flint. However, they already knew how to produce some simple pottery vessels, and the artistic instinct which distinguishes man from even the most intelligent of animals had begun to waken in them, prompting them to carve pieces of bone, wood, and even stone into human, animal, and bird shapes.

A group of settlers inhabiting the eastern shores of Lake Onega, and others living on the shores of the White Sea, began covering the faces of the rocks in these districts with carvings of hunters pursuing their game and with pictures of the local varieties of wild animals—elk, stags, bears, swans, geese, and ducks. One artist even included the figure of a huge demon, which he may perhaps have fancied that he saw one murky night!

These pictures—it would perhaps be better to call them petroglyphs, since the majority were carved on the rocks and only some were actually painted on them—must assuredly have had a magical or religious meaning for the people who produced them, but their original purpose remains unknown to us today. However, certain symbols which later played an important part among early sun worshipers—a form of religion which was popular in various parts of Russia over a long period—already appear in the rock pictures.

More interesting than these sun symbols are scenes throwing some light on the habits of these people by showing them in their narrow boats, intent on harpooning fish, or, aided by their dogs, pursuing animals with spears or shooting at them with bows and arrows. Very similar scenes, done in red paint, have also been found recently in Siberia, notably in Tadjikistan, the Urals, and Central Asia, where they were produced from the third millennium B.C. onward into very early Christian times.

In this period, when the settled inhabitants of the European forest belt and the Ural foothills were still mainly dependent on hunting and fishing, some of the people in the more fertile belt to the south of them had begun to lead an agricultural way of life.

Settling in small groups of tiny mud huts, they worked the land with extremely primitive implements. As still occurs today in certain backward countries, much of this exhausting work was done by the women who toiled beside their menfolk whenever the latter were at home, and carried on alone when the men were away hunting or raiding their weaker neighbors. Under conditions such as these, women came to be regarded as the equals of men, often even as superior to them, so that their word became accepted as law. Societies such as these are called matriarchal, in contrast to the patriarchal in which women lived in servility, while men ruled.

One of the agricultural communities living from about 3000 to 1500 B.C. some forty miles south of Kiev must have been far more advanced than the others. This community produced a culture known today as the Tripolie, which is remarkable for the varied and elaborate shapes of its pottery vessels, some of which have bell-shaped lips and side handles which enabled a rope to be passed through them. Most of these pots were covered with polychrome—many-colored painted decorations formed of spiral or geometric designs, which bear a surprising

Vase of the Tripolie culture decorated with a painted scroll design.

resemblance to those used for a time in ancient Egypt and Crete. Others include the figures of women, dogs, goats, and other animals.

Cattle Breeders

But agriculture in its primitive form could not of itself suffice to meet the growing needs of a developing people, and gradually the more enterprising communities began to think that cattle breeding might provide a more satisfactory form of livelihood. Cattle breeding was, however, far more difficult for a primitive people to practice successfully than the superficial cultivation of small plots of land. In order to rear cattle it was necessary to start by taming the animals concerned; these, depending on the nature of the land, varied from reindeer in the tundra zone, to cattle, sheep, goats, pigs, or horses, in the more southern ones. Next it was necessary for the breeders to provide pastures for their flocks, doing so at a time when the storing of foodstuffs for winter feeding was unknown.

As a result, breeders had to adapt themselves to a nomadic way of life, moving with their families, all their belongings, and their flocks from one piece of pasture land to another. In summer this was easy enough to accomplish in the European section of the plain, for the nomads could generally camp comfortably by a river while their herds roamed the neighboring grasslands. But in winter, when grazing became scarce, many tribes had to travel far afield in search of fodder. Gradually, certain winter grazing grounds came to be recognized as the property of particular groups of people or tribes. When this happened, any attempt by one tribe to trespass on a neighbor's grass became a cause for fierce fighting.

This new way of life was also a more difficult one for women to share in, for it was one in which the men could combine hunting and fishing with the care of their herds. Men were also better fitted to defend their cattle and grazing grounds from raiders, and more adept at raiding their weaker neighbors than were women. Even if the women had wished to share in these pursuits, they could not easily have found the time in which to do so. Living as they did either in tents or in wagons mounted on solid wheels and covered by skin or felt rugs, there was constant packing for them to attend to, in addition to the normal duties of cooking, cleaning, caring for the children and the young and sick animals, milking their beasts, and turning the milk of their herds into a drink called kumis.

Women were also expected to make and repair the family's clothes; to produce most of the felt hangings, cushions, and satchels needed; and probably also to make and decorate the leather reins and many other items of the household's essential equipment. Useful, indeed invaluable, though they were, the women's authority both in the family and in the tribe began to decrease, and by the end of the second millennium B.C. the husband's wish had come to prevail in the family, and the patriarchal system of government to replace the matriarchal in the tribe.

Throughout the vast expanse of the Eurasian plain the nomads and settlers appear to have lived separate lives. As waves of different nomadic groups followed each other, so, in the plain's European section, did a variety of settled agriculturists succeed each other. Each of the agricultural communities could not have greatly differed in their habits, for today each is distinguished only by some slight differences which appear either in the decoration of their equally primitive pottery vessels, or in the construction of their modest mud huts and of the graves which they made for their dead.

Modern archaeologists have grouped them according

to these differences, calling some the Tripolie people because of their pottery. Others they have named the Copper Age people after their pit graves, or Bronze Age communities after their undercut graves and catacomb-like burial chambers. Still other communities are associated with graves of the timber frame type.

In all three types of burial the bodies of the dead were generally laid in their graves in a contracted position, with their legs bent so that their knees were raised close to their chins. The bodies were smeared before burial in a red ochre paint which was thought to have the cleansing effect of fire, and which penetrated to and discolored their bones.

A burial of the pit-grave type known as the Storozhevaya barrow, situated on the right bank of the Dnieper River, contained the oldest cart to have been discovered in Europe. It dated from the third millennium B.C. and was mounted on two immense solid wheels.

Scythian clay model of a nomad's covered wagon.

The nomadic form of existence was more varied and exciting than the monotonous life of the agriculturists, who spent exhausting hours raising indifferent crops with the aid of simple stone implements, or in later times, scarcely less primitive ones of bronze or iron. As a result the nomads were more enterprising and daring, often behaving aggressively and frightening the settled people.

At normal times they would visit the settlements at regular intervals to exchange for grain their meat and fish and animal skins. But when they were short of food they thought nothing of raiding the agriculturists, plundering their villages, kidnaping their children in order to sell them as slaves, and reducing the survivors to a state of absolute obedience. The nomads in this way sometimes gained control over vast agricultural areas, and then they ruthlessly imposed heavy taxes on the terrified farmers in the shape of goods, for money was still unknown to them.

By such means as these, many of their tribal chieftains became rich and powerful. Their wealth is clearly reflected in the variety and splendor of the objects which were placed in their graves, because (like the ancient Egyptians before them) most of the prehistoric inhabitants of the Eurasian plain firmly believed that their dead would continue to need in their life beyond the grave all the things which they had found necessary to their earthly existence.

The graves of the ruling nomadic princes were infinitely more richly furnished than those belonging to the agriculturists. The dead chieftains were buried in their finest clothes, many of which were trimmed with literally dozens of tiny gold plaques decorated with animal or geometric patterns in chased or filigree work. Their war arms were laid within reach of their hands; great quantities of food were provided for them; and their gold cups and other precious vessels, together with their finest objects of silver and bronze, were also buried with them. Little votive ornaments, figures connected with the dead man's religion, were also placed in their graves. These consisted for the most part of small bronze models of bulls or stags.

The Maikop and Trialeti Burials

The richest, and as yet the earliest known royal burial of this type, was that of Maikop in the Kuban. It is dated by present-day Russian scholars to the third millennium B.C. Many precious objects of great artistic quality were found in it, including several superb figures of bulls, some modeled in solid gold and others in bronze, and many tiny gold plaques stamped with figures of lions. Each of these plaques had a small hole in it by means of which it could be stitched to a garment as trimming.

The Maikop grave also contained some beautiful silver and bronze vessels. The most interesting of these is a silver bowl bearing an engraved scene consisting of a mountain range and two rivers, with two groups of

Engraved design on a silver bowl from the Maikop burial.

grazing animals. The outline of the mountain range closely resembles that of the Caucasian mountains when seen from the north, and the peaks appear in the same positions as do in reality those of Elbruz, Ushba, and Kazbek. If the row of hills does indeed represent the Caucasian mountains, then the two rivers on the cup must stand for the Kuban and the Terek. In this case the design on the Maikop bowl is the earliest attempt at a landscape in art that is known to us.

Another group of rather later but scarcely less important princely burials was discovered at Trialeti in Georgia in 1936. Trialeti lies some seventy miles to the southwest of Tbilisi, the capital of the Republic of

Georgia, in the area which the Georgians regard as the cradle of their culture. The tombs belonged to a group of Bronze Age people living there from about 1800 to 1700 B.C., who provided their chieftains with quite elaborate graves. They were entered by a shaft which was generally filled in with stones after the burial had taken place. The burial chamber was at the far end of the shaft, and contained at its center a heavy four-wheeled cart bearing the ashes of the chieftain's cremated body. The carcasses of the goats and other animals which had been killed to provide him with food in his afterlife were piled around the cart. Numerous pottery vessels, in some cases as many as two dozen, were included. Some of these were colored red or yellow and were decorated with brown or black painted designs; others were black, and had incised designs which had been filled in with a red substance.

The people of the Trialeti burials had reached a transitional phase in man's development, for although they were sufficiently advanced to possess some bronze tools they were still at the stage of using flint arrowheads instead of metal ones. Their wealth was reflected in the chieftain's personal possessions, which consisted of numerous objects in gold and silver, including a silver dagger. Of exceptional artistic quality is a large gold cup decorated with filigree work and set with turquoises, agates, and semiprecious red stones.

A particularly fine silver beaker has a handle adorned with a hunting scene. Most interesting of all is a goblet

Map of European Russia showing some of the more important early burials and medieval towns.

decorated with two scenes fitted into two horizontal bands and carried out in chased work. The lower scene shows a procession of stags solemnly advancing in single file; the upper presents a series of human beings with animal heads and tails, advancing in single file in the opposite direction to that of the stags to present offerings to a chieftain or some deity seated in front of a sacrificial tree. Both scenes are probably connected with a religious ceremony, and the masks and tails worn by the human beings must have had much the same meaning in their day as do similar masks still used in semireligious ceremonies in certain remote parts of Africa.

The discovery of objects such as these in the Caucasus, the Kuban valley, or western Siberia prove both by their numbers and their technical excellence that by the third millennium B.C., people living in these areas had learned to use metals. Their ability to do so naturally depended upon available supplies, but these must not have been difficult to obtain, for the regions in which they lived are still rich in mineral deposits today. Since they appear to have had adequate supplies of the metals they needed, it is reasonable to suppose that they had discovered how to mine them. This in turn makes it possible for us to assert that it was these people who took the first step toward establishing what has grown into the science of metallurgy. Nevertheless, the knowledge they had acquired did not become generally known throughout the Caucasus and Siberia until the second millennium B.C., and it was not fully mastered by the inhabitants of the southwestern, western, and northern areas of what is now European Russia until the first millennium B.C.

The finds from Maikop and Trialeti also serve to show that the animal style in art (the home of which lies in ancient Egypt, Mesopotamia, and Persia) had already established itself in the Caucasian and west-Siberian areas by the third millennium B.C. It may well be that certain elements in the style had originated in the latter areas, doing so at a time so remote that we as yet know very little about it.

In the far-distant past Eskimos living in the tundra belt were fond of carving whalebone into fish and other animal shapes. They may have taught their neighbors in the forest belt to do likewise, and these in their turn may have introduced some elements of the animal style into ancient Persia. But whatever its origins, the animal style in decorative art was to reach superb heights in the hands of the nomadic horse breeders of Scythian and related origins who roamed the Eurasian plain in the first millennium B.C.

The Age of the Nomads

IT WAS in the Late Bronze Age that the first important group of nomads crossed into Europe from Asia to settle in what is now southern Russia. Their cultured contemporaries in Persia called them Cimmerians, and it may well be they who gave the Crimea its present name, for the ancient Greeks called the Straits of Kerch the Cimmerian Bosphorus.

The newcomers lived by breeding cattle and horses, eating the flesh and drinking the milk of their beasts. They traveled on foot or in carts, since they had not as yet discovered how to ride the horse. Very few of their graves have so far been examined, and those which have been opened have for the most part contained objects which are not valuable in themselves. But although the

Cimmerians do not appear to have been wealthy, they nevertheless succeeded in gaining control of most of the south Russian plain, retaining it for several centuries.

THE SCYTHIANS

History, the study of written documents, as distinct from pre-history, when our knowledge depends on the archaeological information obtained from studying objects, begins in so far as Russia is concerned about 800 B.C. It was then that Persian chroniclers started to record the appearance on Persia's northern borders of a new group of nomads. Instead of *driving* horses, as all had done before them, these adventurous newcomers actually *rode* them. They are known to us today as the Scythians. Together with groups of other Asiatic tribesmen who were perhaps related to them and who in any case resembled them, they concentrated on breeding horses in preference to, rather than to the exclusion of, other animals.

The Egyptians and the ancient Persians, as well as the early Greeks, had all made use of the horse for years before the Scythians appeared on the northern borders of Persia, but they had used them only in harness, to pull carts in peace time and chariots in time of war. Most of their horses they obtained from nomadic breeders similar to the Scythians who had raised horses as much for their meat, milk, and hides as for transport. But it was the Scythians who, having first lassoed their horses, were

Above: *part of a frieze on the Chertomlyk Vase showing Scythians breaking and saddling their horses.* **Below:** *full view of the Chertomlyk Vase, fourth century* B.C.

among the first people (possibly even the very first) to learn to lunge them on a long rein just as we do today. Then, they began to use a snaffle bit which scarcely differs from the modern one, and taught the horse to respond to the rein and finally to carry, first a saddle and then a man.

The process is shown in all its detail on the frieze decorating the splendid electrum vessel found in a royal burial of the fourth century B.C. at Chertomlyk in southern Russia, even to the inclusion of the fabric footrest suspended from one of the saddles, for metal stirrups had not yet been invented. It is known today as the Chertomlyk vase. Though the vase is unlikely to have been made by a Scythian—it is probably the work of a Greek jeweler—it must have been commissioned by a Scythian, for only a Scythian would have been sufficiently interested in the training of horses to wish to see the process rendered on a vase, and only a Scythian could have furnished all the information and details of style in dress and saddling that were essential to the artist.

The Scythians were an Iranian people who had for centuries lived at the eastern end of the Eurasian plain. Sometime in the ninth century B.C. their eastern neighbors, tribesmen who were later to appear in western Europe as the Huns, had begun to raid the peaceful peasants of western China, causing them so much worry that eventually the Chinese emperor Suan (827–781 B.C.) decided to send an army to punish them.

The well-disciplined Chinese troops did not content

themselves with evicting the Huns from Chinese territory, but proceeded to push them quite far back into the plain. By doing so, they upset the balance of power in the area, for the retreating Huns seized the grazing grounds of the tribes living to the west of them, and these in their turn took up arms against their immediate neighbors to their west, who did likewise, until the whole Asiatic section of the plain was in a turmoil. As a result, the Scythians found themselves being pushed westward by tribesmen in search of new pastures. Packing their belongings, they mounted their horses and moved southwestward, till they eventually overflowed into northern Persia.

The ability to ride gave the Scythians the great advantage of speed in attack. They made the most of it, using mounted archers who showered their enemies with arrows while attacking them from several directions. They were proud, obedient, and altogether fearless fighters; and they succeeded in completely routing the Cimmerians, making them flee from southern Russia into Persia and pushing them back across what is today eastern Turkey until they had completely destroyed them.

For some twenty-eight years the Scythians retained control over the sections of northeastern Persia and Turkey through which the Cimmerians had retreated. Then they lost their advantage of being the only mounted horsemen in the region. The people of the occupied countries had quickly learned to ride, and the commanders of the Parthians who were settled in southern Asia Minor and northern Mesopotamia had been able to add some cavalry units to their regiments so that they were strong enough to challenge the Scythians.

In a series of well-conducted campaigns around the middle of the eighth century B.C. the Parthians succeeded fairly quickly in evicting the Scythians from Persian territory, allowing them to depart on the promise of a payment of an annual tribute. That the promise was kept, at any rate for a time, is shown by a frieze in the great Persian palace of Persepolis where Scythians appear beside the tribute bearers from other vanquished people.

Some of the Scythians who were evicted by the Persians found themselves pushed back into Urartu—a kingdom which extended over what is known today as Armenia, with the addition of the district in and around Lake Van in present-day eastern Turkey. Urartu had been a flourishing and prosperous kingdom from the ninth century B.C.

It was also a civilized country, one in which the learned used a cuneiform (wedge-shaped) script to write in, where the wealthy slaveowners lived in comfortable, well-furnished houses, and where agricultural workers raised good crops of barley, wheat, millet, beans, and lentils, and also made wines from the grapes in their vineyards.

The excavations which have been carried out within the last few years on the great citadel of Karmir Blur, situated quite close to Armenia's modern capital Erevan,

Gold casing from a wooden carving of a lion of the ninth century B.C. *from Karmir Blur* (courtesy B. B. Piotrowski)

make it clear that the Urartians also had a highly organized army. The citadel consisted of a hundred and twenty rooms enclosed within stout defensive walls. Among many other things the excavators found there the helmet of the Urartian king Argistis. It is made of bronze and is magnificently decorated with a design consisting of eleven sacred trees with, at its center, the figure of a winged god wearing a horned headdress and guarded on either side by lion-headed dragons. A chariot and horsemen armed with round shields and spears complete the decoration. The horsemen prove that the Urartians had wasted little time in learning to ride, but their ability to do so was not to save them from the Scythians.

When the Scythians who were retreating across Urartu attacked the garrison of Karmir Blur, the fighting was so fierce, and was carried on at such close range, that some of the Scythian trefoil arrowheads remain embedded to this day in the ruined walls of the fortress. No written account of the battle survives, but the excavations have shown that the Scythians conquered the citadel by throwing lighted firebrands on its roofing of wood and twigs, and once these had caught fire nothing could save the structure.

The fall of Karmir Blur proved disastrous to Urartu. The kingdom never recovered from it, and in 585 B.C. the Medes had little difficulty in putting an end to its existence. However, surviving Urartians continued to cling to their homes and their native land until they eventually reappeared in history as the Georgian and Armenian kingdoms of early Christian times.

Having passed through Urartu, the Scythians dallied for a time in the Kuban valley, where they were probably joined by other groups of Scythians who had crossed into Europe by different routes. Some of the earliest and richest royal Scythian burials have been found in the Kuban. They are remarkable for the artistic quality of the numerous gold, silver, and bronze objects in them. Many of these are decorated with designs in which the influence of Persian art is clearly to be seen.

The bulk of the Scythians did not settle in the Kuban. Many of them pushed on into southern Russia, where they established themselves as the rulers of the section of the plain which lies between the rivers Don and Bug. There, though living as nomads, they became so powerful that, in the sixth century B.C., they were able to defy the mighty Persian leader Darius when he penetrated into Scythia in an attempt to advance to the Volga; indeed, they forced him to retreat to the Danube's basin.

They were still so powerful in the fourth century B.C. that they caused considerable concern to Alexander the Great. In fact, from the sixth to about the third century B.C., their international importance was so impressive that Herodotus, the fifth century B.C. Greek scholar who has been aptly called the "Father of History," considered it essential to devote a whole chapter in his history to giving an account of them. To be able to do so satisfactorily, Herodotus crossed the Black Sea to spend several months in the Greek coastal city of Olbia to study the Scythians at first hand. Present-day excavations have confirmed the correctness of much of what he wrote about them.

Though the bulk of the Royal Scyths lived on the grasslands bordering the lower Dnieper, others spread farther afield, some spilling southward into the Crimea and the hinterland of the Sea of Azov—without, however, occupying any of the coastline. Subsidiary tribes, whose names were recorded by Herodotus, settled in neighboring areas. All of them, as well as groups of nomads living in western Siberia, and more particularly in the Altaian foothills, followed the Scythian way of life and practiced the Scythian type of decorative art.

Although the number of Royal Scyths was probably considerably smaller than that of the settlers living in the European section of the plain, it was the Scythians who were masters of the area. They roamed it in their covered wagons, occasionally perhaps sleeping in tents, breeding and breaking in their horses, fishing and hunting, trading their surplus wares for the agricultural products offered by the settlers, bartering all they could spare with their neighbors.

A little of their trade was with China; more of it was with Persia, and both direct and through Persian middlemen, with Mesopotamia, Greece, Asia Minor, Thrace, and Pannonia (between the Danube and the Alps). Most of it, however, was conducted with the Greek colonials living in self-governing towns situated along the northern shores of the Black Sea, in what is today known as southern Russia. The ancient Greeks called this region the Euxine Pontus, *Pontus Euxinus,* Latin for "sea" and "black."

These Greek colonials quickly came to depend upon the Scythians for the bulk of their food supplies, and more especially for the grain which the Scythians levied from the settlers and bartered to the Greeks for such luxuries as jewelry or finely painted pottery. The grain trade was an especially important one, because Greece proper, which could no longer feed itself, looked to the Greeks of the Euxine Pontus for the bulk of their needs.

The Scythians had no alphabet, and so could neither read nor write; nor did they have a coinage, until much later in their history. They were not deeply religious, though they believed in a number of gods, and more particularly in a Great Goddess. They occasionally offered sacrifices to one or another of these divinities, but they never built any temples and they preferred to put their faith in their own magicians rather than in their gods. One advantage of this was that they could punish any sorcerer who had been proved wrong by having him put to death, whereas a god would have had to be excused.

Scythian Burials

Instead of worshiping deities the Scythians venerated the graves of their notables, sparing neither trouble nor expense to provide their leaders with sumptuous burials. A chieftain's funeral was an extremely elaborate and astonishingly costly affair—costly not only in material objects but in human and animal lives.

The tombs were so elaborate in construction that they took several weeks to build. While part of the tribe were employed in making the grave, the rest placed the body of their dead master on a cart and—some carrying his standard and spear, others wailing and tearing their clothes and their hair—marched in procession through the dead man's territory, daily collecting more and more of his people until all his subjects had been assembled for the funeral.

Meanwhile the gravediggers had begun by constructing a shaft or ramp, looking like a roofed-in corridor, leading to the spot chosen for the burial chamber. According to its geographical situation, the burial consisted of either a single chamber or of a central one with as many as four compartments radiating from it. The burial chambers were generally lined with logs and, depending on the locality, hung with either wicker or rush matting. They were roofed either with birch bark or thatch. Sometimes, as in the later Crimean tombs, the entire inner structure was made of great stone slabs, on some of which traces of mural paintings still survive.

All the Scythian burials were horse burials. Some of the best horses which had belonged to the dead man were killed at his funeral and buried in their finest trappings beside their master. Their harness consisted of snaffle bits, cheek pieces and headbands, all of which were elaborately decorated with animal designs carried out in gold leaf, bronze or wood. Over the ages, the saddles and harness pieces disintegrated, but their gold leaf decorations have survived to this day.

The poorest graves contained only one horse, while the richest sometimes held as many as several hundred, though twelve to fifty was a more usual number. The chieftain's body always occupied the central position in the main burial chamber. He was placed in it wearing

Scythian dagger, 20 inches long, from the Chertomlyk burial, fifth to fourth century B.C. *The gold hilt is decorated with animal designs.*

his finest clothes, many of which were trimmed with innumerable little gold plaques of the same type, though decorated with different designs, as those belonging to the Maikop ruler. Often a spare set of clothing was hung on a peg fixed to one of the walls. All of the man's jewels, his necklaces, arm and ankle rings, bracelets, finger rings, pins and buckles, and often a gold skull cap, were placed in position on his body.

The arms which he had used in battle were also laid within his reach. These consisted of a sword of the Scythian type which was often provided with a sheath of chased gold, and a bow of the compounded Asiatic sort, which was designed for the use of horsemen and was kept in a beautifully ornamented case, known as a gorytus, which was specially arranged to hold both the bow and arrows. Daggers of the Persian type often mounted into ornate handles were usual, as were knives—many of which were curved like Chinese ones, helmets of Greek or local make, and jerkins of chain or scale armor. Gold goblets and cups to which the Scyths attached particular importance were also placed in the graves, and often also ceremonial axes made of semiprecious materials were included.

Quantities of food and wine were provided. Essential to every burial was the inclusion of a huge bronze cauldron, mounted on a tripod foot or base for standing over a fire.

The Scythians and their kindred tribesmen were so firmly convinced that their dead would lead exactly the same sort of life in the world beyond the grave as they had done in this, that they never hesitated to kill one of the dead man's wives in order that she should accompany him to the world beyond. The Royal Scyths killed in addition the head servants of their notables—their head grooms, their cupbearers, and their chief cooks. Like their masters, all these dead were buried in their best clothes, wearing their finest jewelry, and surrounded by their essential possessions which, in the case of women, included a bronze mirror.

When everything necessary had been placed in the tomb, the grave was sealed and the bodies of the dead horses piled around it. Then the solid-wheeled carts which had been used in the funeral procession were broken up and the pieces placed in the grave's entrance shaft. Only when this had been done was a great mound of earth raised over the tomb. Then all those who had attended the funeral gathered on the mound to partake of the great feast which was held there to commemorate the dead.

The first important Scythian burial in southern Russia, the Melgunov barrow in the Dnieper area, was discovered as far back as 1763. Its contents astonished

A chased gold figure of a stag, about 12 inches high, probably once the central ornament on a Scythian shield. From the Kostromskaya barrow in the Kuban, seventh to sixth century B.C.

antiquarians. In particular they were amazed by the splendor of the gold sword sheath decorated in the Assyrian style, and the magnificence of a gold diadem adorned with onyx and the gold figures of birds and animals.

Some of the richest barrows were excavated in the course of the nineteenth century. Many were in the Kuban, and in these the profusion of gold and silver objects was so great that it served to explain why the Greeks believed that Jason had set out to seek the Golden Fleece in the Kuban, which was known to them as Colchis. Among the loveliest objects which have been recovered from the royal burials are the figures of gold stags which originally formed the central decorations on the round shields carried by some Scyths.

Three of these stags, including the splendid seventh to sixth century B.C. example found in the Kostromskaya barrow in the Kuban, are outstanding. In all of them the stag is shown in such a way that it appears to be both lying down resting, and also galloping at great speed. This double impression is achieved by showing the animal with its legs tucked under it, while its head, and occasionally also its forelegs, are raised as if in rapid motion. Although no animal could in life assume such a position, the Scythian plaques are so carefully thought out, and the modeling is so true to life, that the finished work is thoroughly convincing.

Scarcely less fine are the figures of gold leopards and other animals, some of the bronze versions of which show the beast turned into a circle. Hundreds of the little gold plaques used as dress trimmings were decorated with chased or embossed animal designs, in which griffins and members of the cat family frequently recur. On other objects animals are often shown in what is known as the flying gallop—a position which the Scythians were particularly fond of representing.

The Scythians' ability and their delight in recreating the animal form in all its numerous and varied aspects produced certain other peculiarities in their art. Foremost among these is the habit of taking part of one creature, such as its tail or a stag's antlers, and either putting it onto the head of another or developing it into a

Decoration from the Melgunov gold sword sheath illustrating an unusual combination of animal figures. Seventh to sixth century B.C.

series of extremely complicated shapes, often of an animal character. The resulting picture is, of course, always untrue to life, yet it seems so real that it does not look like an imaginary creation but rather the picture of some extinct prehistoric beast or some real creature of which we as yet know nothing.

The Scythians were particularly fond of showing animals, both real and imaginary, locked in fight in such a way that the shapes formed by their bodies produced curved outlines. They were also in the habit of indicating the muscles on an animal's body by dot and comma markings, and of giving most of their birds the great beaks which belong to eagles and hawks. Indeed, their animal art, with its blend of realism and abstraction, is one which is particularly suited to our taste today, molded as it has been by the works of such contemporary artists as Picasso.

At the turn of the seventeenth century, in the reign of Peter the Great, a considerable number of people from western Russia started moving to Siberia to earn their living there. Many of them were surprised by the large number of burial mounds which they noticed; and some of the more daring of the newcomers could not resist tunneling into an occasional barrow and penetrating into the rich burials which lay concealed within. Among the objects which these treasure hunters discovered were some gold and bronze belt buckles formed of animals, often shown intertwined and decorated with semi-precious stones and enamel inlays.

The finds were reported to Peter the Great, who gave orders for all the metal plaques to be bought and sent to him, and forbade all further looting. When the collection, consisting of some two hundred and seventy objects, reached the Czar he displayed it in his Cabinet of

Cast bronze ornament for a horse, from the Kuban, fourth century B.C. It is about 6 inches wide, and the stag's head in the center has antlers which terminate in the heads of birds.

Curios, from which it later passed to the Hermitage Museum in St. Petersburg, now Leningrad. There it aroused the interest of visitors, many of whom noticed a close resemblance between the Siberian plaques and similar objects recovered from the Scythian burials of southern Russia. Curiously enough, however, no archaeologists began to study the Siberian burials until 1865, when a scholar called Radlov started excavating at Katanda, a burial ground situated on the southern slopes of the western Altai mountain range.

Unlike southern Russia, where the mounds which were raised above the Scythian burials were made of earth, those at Katanda had been topped with a layer of boulders so that the size of a mound depended upon its circumference and not its height. Radlov removed the boulders from the mound he had decided to examine, and his men had been digging for only a short time when they were astonished to find their progress stopped by a layer of ice. Its appearance there was inexplicable, since Katanda is situated well outside the zone of perpetual ice. Radlov was at a loss to account for it below the level of the boulders, and he was never to know that he had stumbled upon the first of what are now known as the frozen tombs of the Altai. In these tombs the ice was produced by the rain water which had filtered through the boulders and loose earth covering a newly made grave, and had frozen during the bitterly cold winter months. It never melted again because, even during the short though hot summers, the boulders insulated it from the sun's rays. As a result, everything within these tombs has remained preserved as if in a modern deep freeze.

Radlov was so unprepared for the ice that he failed to prevent some of it melting before it could be properly dealt with. Water penetrated into the tomb and spoiled part of its contents. Radlov was, nevertheless, able to recover many objects of the kind which usually survive only in the dry climate and sandy soil of Egypt, and which have generally perished in Russian burials. Among his discoveries were several articles of clothing. One garment, though some two thousand years old, was cut on exactly the same lines as a Regency tail coat.

For some inexplicable reason, however, none of Radlov's finds, for all their exciting novelty, succeeded in arousing the curiosity of his contemporaries, and no one continued the work he had begun in Siberia.

It was not until 1924 that interest in that distant region revived as a result of an archaeological survey undertaken there on behalf of the U.S.S.R. State Ethnographical Society by the scholars Rudenko and Griasnov. In the course of their travels their attention was drawn to the burial ground of Pazyryk, situated in a valley of the western Altai, somewhat to the north of Katanda. In 1929 they were able to start excavating one of the largest mounds. They found that it too was sealed off from the outer world by a layer of ice similar to that which Radlov had encountered at Katanda. Indeed, it was Rudenko who discovered that the ice is peculiar to the boulder-covered burials of the Altaian region.

Rudenko has so far been able to open six of the Pazyryk burials. He has dealt with them so skillfully that he has succeeded in preserving all the innumerable and varied objects which he found in them exactly as he saw them for the first time when he peered through a chink in the ice covering Mound 1. As he gazed through this gap he saw, as in a peep show, a microcosm or tiny replica of a nomad's world some two thousand years old. All his finds are now exhibited in the Hermitage Museum at Leningrad. His discovery has not only revealed a civilization, the very existence of which was unknown to us before, but it has also supplied us with much detailed information about its way of life.

The Pazyryk burials belonged to a nomadic people who lived in the area from the fifth to the second century B.C. and whose culture is so very similar to that of the Scythians of southern Russia that they may well be regarded as kindred tribesmen. They were, however, far less advanced than the Royal Scyths, and were a poorer people, even though they also lived by raising herds of horses and cattle.

Their tombs do not contain nearly as many objects made in valuable materials as the Royal Scythian tombs, though the scarcity of precious articles may partly be due to the fact that all the burials so far uncovered by Rudenko had been looted long ago, probably soon after the funerals had taken place. Nevertheless, a number of gold leaf decorations have been recovered from them.

The great fascination of the Pazyryk burials is due to the discovery in them of the precise types of perishable objects which failed to survive in the climatic and soil conditions of southern Russia. Since the metal and bone objects found at Pazyryk are very similar to objects of the same sort discovered in southern Russia, it can safely be assumed that the objects of a perishable nature recovered from the Pazyryk burials also resembled articles of a similar kind in use among the Royal Scyths. Thus the knowledge derived from the Altaian burials not only throws light on conditions in that area but fills gaps in what had previously been known about the Scyths of Russia.

The Pazyryk tombs were reached by a shaft, opening into two adjoining chambers similarly lined with logs which had been smoothed on the inner sides to look like walls and hung with textiles. Their earth floors were either paved with wood or beaten flat and sometimes covered with gravel, and their ceilings were generally made of birch bark laid on wooden rafters. All contained horse burials of the Scythian type, but whereas in southern Russia the carcasses of the horses were piled around the outside of the human tomb, at Pazyryk they were all laid in the northernmost and slightly smaller of the two chambers, though this was decorated in exactly the same way as the human burial chamber.

At Pazyryk the bodies both of people and horses were admirably preserved by the frozen condition of their tombs. The dead men and women were buried in individual log coffins, some of which were decorated on the outside with splendid animal carvings. They included the body of a man who had been tattooed all over with a magnificent series of fantastic, superbly drawn animal designs executed in the Scythian style. Some of the beasts appearing on his body were entirely imaginary, some real; most were shown interlocked in fierce combats drawn with very graceful outlines. Among the dead horses were found the bodies of some thoroughbred Ferghanas, which were so much valued that they had been wintered under cover and fed by hand, whereas the others, rough Mongolian ponies, had had to fend for

Repeat motif in appliqué felt from a large wall hanging of the fifth century* B.C., *found in Mound 5, Pazyryk.

Section of the Persian woolen pile carpet of the fifth century B.C. found in Mound 5, Pazyryk.

themselves during the cold, almost fodderless season.

The clothes were of the tight-fitting sort suited to people living an outdoor life in a harsh climate—thick cloaks worn over jerkins, hoods, thick stockings and bootees; a variety of satchels and purses was also found. All were made of fur, leather, or felt, and each object was profusely trimmed with vividly colored, amazingly complicated designs carried out in appliqué felts. They comprised figural scenes, animal designs, and geometric patterns which included symbols of the Sun cult.

Each of the Pazyryk burials contained a tripod-legged cauldron of the Scythian type. The household furniture

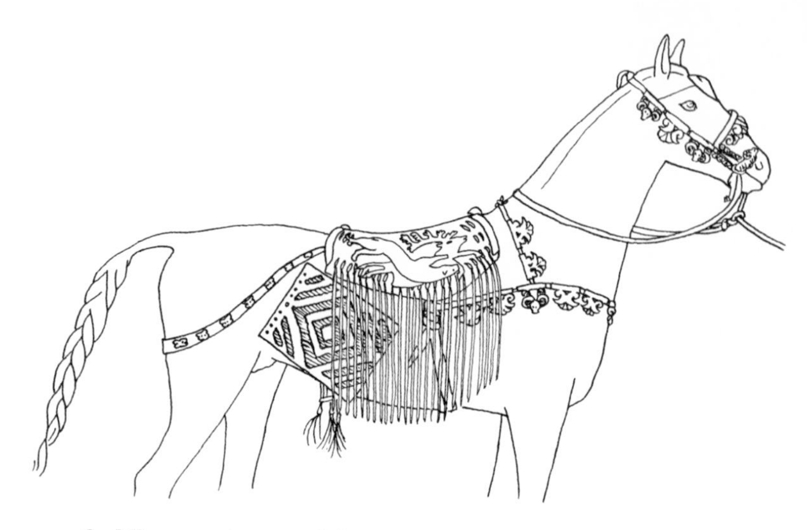

Saddle, trappings, and harness belonging to a horse buried in Mound 1, Pazyryk, fifth to third century B.C.

consisted of wooden blocks which served both as stools and as headrests, small tables with detachable traylike tops mounted on turned legs, often finished off with carvings of lions' heads, and a mass of cooking utensils. Felt hangings were widely used. One immensely large one was decorated with a repeat scene of a seated goddess granting an audience to a mounted warrior, while a smaller one shows a rather frightening semihuman, semianimal creature.

However, perhaps the most interesting discovery of all was made in Mound 5 where the world's oldest, virtually complete carpet was found. It is a Persian woolen pile rug made in the same knotted technique that is in use in Persia today. But its design is characteristic of its own time and consists of stars, figures of griffins, a procession of elk, and another in which riders and grooms are leading splendidly caparisoned horses.

All the horse trappings found at Pazyryk are as highly decorated as the belongings of their human masters. A well-turned-out horse carried an ornamented felt saddle cloth, over which rested a soft saddle made of two flat felt cushions mounted on a wooden frame. This was sometimes decorated with embossed gold plaques. The bridles, snaffles, and head and cheek pieces were of the Scythian types, and were similarly decorated with either embossed, cut out, or carved animal and geometric forms, including figures of cocks very similar to those which recur in Russian folk art from early times down to our own day.

Felt and leather headdress mask for a horse from Mound 2, Pazyryk, fifth century B.C.

In addition, several of the best bred horses were provided with extraordinary masks. One was in the form of a ram's head and was surmounted with the figure of a falcon, while another was made out of a reindeer's skull and antlers. Indeed, elk, stags, and reindeer appear so frequently in both Altaian and Scythian art that it seems more than likely that they possessed some sort of religious meaning for the tribesmen. At one stage of their history these nomads in fact believed that animals of the reindeer family were able to carry the dead to the world beyond the grave far more quickly than could any other creature.

In the later Scythian period, griffins, leopards, and other members of the cat family, as well as lions, rams, bulls, and wolves, figure in their art as often as do stags. On the other hand the horse, the very animal on which the nomads depended for their well-being, scarcely ever appears in it—a most surprising omission, which cannot as yet be satisfactorily explained.

Like prehistoric man, the Eurasian nomads lived in such close touch with the animal world that they knew as much about it as they did about their fellow men. They also lived at a time when craftsmanship was so highly developed that it attained to true art, and the Scythian and kindred tribes of the Eurasian plain produced not merely a characteristic type of decoration, not even a personal style, but a veritable school in art. The beauty of this school is only now beginning to be widely appreciated.

Greek Cities on the Black Sea

WHILE THE Scythians were fighting their way across Urartu to the western section of the Eurasian plain, lack of grain, together with certain other economic and political needs, induced some of the independent city states of ancient Greece to found colonies, mainly in the eastern Mediterranean area.

The ancient Greeks were an adventurous and seafaring people, and in the eighth century B.C. some of their sailors, perhaps encouraged by the story of Jason's adventures in Colchis, found their way into the Black Sea while searching for cheap slaves for the Greek markets. They eventually reached the Sea's eastern and northern shores, and were soon after followed by Greek merchants who founded offices which came to be called factories along what is today the south-Russian coast.

By the seventh century B.C. some of these factories had grown into veritable colonial outposts, and by the fifth century B.C. practically the whole of the northern shore of the Black Sea, especially the ports at the mouths of the great rivers which flow into it, had been fully colonized by the Greeks. They had also settled along the coast of the Sea of Azov.

These colonials carried on a lively trade with their homeland, but they remained content to develop only the coastal areas of Russia, and to draw the barbarians—as they called the nomads and settlers living in the plain behind them—to their markets. As a result, the Greeks never penetrated into the plain, though they came to depend almost entirely on it for their supplies of grain, fish, meat, honey, and furs—goods which the Scythians either produced or obtained from their settled subjects.

The most prosperous of the Greek colonial cities were Olbia, situated on the Bug and Dnieper estuaries; Tanais on the estuary of the Don; and Phanagoria on the Taman peninsula. The Crimea was also widely colonized by the Greeks, and the flourishing city of Chersonesus sprang up close to present-day Sebastopol. Near it, on the site of modern Kerch, rose the city of Panticapaeum. Soon the whole Black Sea coastline of southern and eastern Russia consisted of a narrow belt of semi-independent Greek city-states.

Although the majority of the Greek colonial cities have been examined by Russian archaeologists, it is Olbia, together with Chersonesus and Panticapaeum which have been most extensively excavated. Olbia was the oldest of these cities, having been founded in the seventh century B.C. as a colony of the Greek city-state Miletus. It quickly became a self-governing republic based on a system of slavery. It was first excavated in 1801; but it was not until a hundred years later, when the eminent archaeologist Farmakovsky became interested in its ruins, that work started on a large scale.

Excavations were conducted there annually until the outbreak of World War I. They were resumed in 1928 and continued until 1936, and as a result a great deal is now known both about Olbia itself and also about the sort of life which was led in the other colonial cities.

Olbia

Olbia was at its most prosperous during the fifth and much of the fourth century B.C. when it covered a triangular area bordered on the one side by the river Bug and on the other by a sort of natural moat. A great wall surrounded it to afford additional protection—in places this wall was as much as twelve feet thick. A very wide main street ran down the center of the town, cutting it in two, the side streets joining it at right angles. Open canals flowed along the sides of the streets, bringing water to the inhabitants. As was usual in ancient times, the upper town was more important than the lower, and the agora, or market place, was therefore situated in it.

The main temple stood at the center of the agora, and around it were the best buildings in the town. In these the ground floors were turned into shops, their owners using the basements as storerooms, while the upper floors contained government offices.

The most important houses were built of dressed stone set in alternate layers of clay and earth, and were roofed with tiles. Many were adorned with sculptured or plastered decorations. It may have been the sight of these which so enchanted Scyles, one of the earlier kings of the Royal Scyths, that he could not resist acquiring a similar house for himself, even though he knew that by doing so he would rouse the fierce resentment of his people.

Scyles thus became the first Scythian to live in a house instead of a tent. He tried to keep this a secret, but he was eventually killed by his own bodyguard, who were angered by his fondness for Greek customs.

Olbia's less grand houses were given stone foundations, but their walls were built of baked bricks. The town's cemetery was a large one, situated outside the walls. Its later graves include Scythian burials among the Greek ones—a sign that some of the nomads had, like Scyles before them, been won over by the Greek way of life. Links between the Greeks and the Scythians appear to have been close from the start, for although the type of art practiced at Olbia remained basically Greek with a touch of Egyptian influence, strong Scythian elements also appear in it.

Olbia was from its very beginning a commercial city.

How the Scythian designs persisted through the centuries: on the left, a cock from a fifth century B.C. *leather flagon found at Pazyryk; on the right, a cock embroidered on an eighteenth century bed curtain in Nizhni Novgorod.*

In addition to sending Scythian grain to Miletus, it imported from Rhodes great amphorae, or jugs, filled with wine. It also traded with Pharos, Pergamon, Alexandria, and many towns in Asia Minor, especially with Sinop, situated on the opposite shore of the Black Sea in what is now Turkey. Olbia minted its own coinage, using it for its trade with Greece, but it exchanged superb Greek vases, jewelry, and other imported luxuries with the Scythians, who still did not use money.

Olbia's eastern trade was as important as her trade with Greece, and, until late into the fourth century B.C., the town served as the starting point for caravans heading for the Volga and the Urals. Many of these caravans carried goods which had been made in Olbia's own workshops. Chief among them were textiles, rather coarse pottery vessels, and jewelry of fine quality which was produced in great quantities. Some of the better Olbian pottery was made on the wheel, and was decorated with Scythian designs very similar to those which appear on the metal objects which have been recovered from the town's Scythian burials.

Chersonesus

Chersonesus appears to have been a richer town than Olbia; it was certainly larger, and was probably the biggest of all the Greek colonial cities. It was founded in 421 B.C. by emigrants from Heraclea-Pontica, a town on the southern shore of the Black Sea. They established themselves on land which belonged to the Tauri tribe, a branch of the Cimmerians who had survived in the Crimea and given the region the name of Tauride.

Like Olbia, Chersonesus was also a slave-owning, self-governing, republican city—a fact which is known to us because of the discovery in its ruins of the oath which its freemen had to swear to. Like Olbia, it was laid out on rectangular lines; like Olbia, it struck its own coinage, which it used for carrying on trade of a similar type. However, unlike Olbia, Chersonesus gradually succeeded in extending its hold over much of the neighboring coastline, and it eventually became the capital of the western Crimea. Its Greek population mingled with the native Tauri inhabitants, with the result that local traditions came to blend with the imported Greek ones. Thus, whereas the Greek god Heraclius was the one most widely worshiped, some Scythian and Tauri deities were also venerated in Chersonesus.

Most of the Tauri were by now farming the land lying outside the city's walls, providing the town dwellers with a steady flow of fresh food supplies. Many of the city people became rich enough to decorate their houses with fine mosaic floors, mural paintings and sculptures, as well as to buy for themselves much lovely jewelry. They were fond of wearing ear and finger rings as well as gold torques (collars made of twisted gold wires), gold anklets, fibulae or pins, and buckles of various sorts. Much of their jewelry came from Attica and Thrace, and much more from Asia Minor, but a good deal was also made locally. Many of the objects were decorated with chased or filigree work as well as with inset jewels and

Gold necklace of Scythian design found at Kerch in Southern Russia (from the Ashmolean Museum, Oxford)

enamel fillings, and some of the locally made pieces were adorned with scenes from Scythian life. Nor were the children forgotten; excavators have found toys among the ruins, including balls, knuckle bones, and even dolls' tea sets.

PANTICAPAEUM

Panticapaeum was also essentially a commercial town, but conditions there differed slightly from those at Olbia and Chersonesus, for Panticapaeum chose to become a monarchy instead of a republic. Founded sometime in the sixth century B.C., it was at its most prosperous from the fourth to the third century B.C. Then the bulk of the people were traders, and many of them lived as veritable merchant princes. However, they also devoted some of their time to managing the farms they acquired in the country and to military duties.

To regular soldiers the army offered considerable scope for promotion, for there were always either raiding Asiatic nomads, wild Scythian chieftains, or neighboring colonial cities to fight against. Panticapaeum eventually succeeded in conquering so many of these that it became the capital of the Taman area; but although it sometimes fought the Scythians, it was on the whole on good terms with many of them.

Both profited from their trading agreements, and the Scythian burials in the Crimea are among the richest and most splendid of all the later ones. The tombs which were built near Panticapaeum from the fourth century B.C. onward are extremely elaborate and impressive. The most remarkable is the Tsarsky (meaning Royal) burial in the district of Kerch, which is so high a building that its outlines are visible from a great distance.

It was built of huge blocks of stone; and its vast size, superb proportions, and excellent masonry work produce such an overwhelming effect on visitors that, as late as the mid-nineteenth century, many a traveler assumed it to be the burial place of the Pontic emperor, Mithridates Eupator. It consisted of a tall, narrow hall leading to a rectangular burial chamber roofed with a barrel vaulted ceiling.

Burials of the same type, though of smaller dimensions, continued to be built in the Taman peninsula until about the second century A.D. Their walls and ceilings were often covered with very attractive wall paintings. The most interesting to us today are those which include the figures of mounted horsemen, especially when they are shown fighting with nomadic raiders.

The Struggle over Southern Russia

IN ABOUT the fourth century B.C., at a time when the Greek colonial cities were thriving and the Scythians were contentedly spending their days in the western section of the Eurasian plain, another upheaval among the tribes living in its Asiatic region disrupted the peace of the inhabitants of southern Russia. The Huns, who had already been responsible for the Scythian invasion of Europe, had once again been disturbed by the Chinese and had begun to move toward Mongolia.

Excavations undertaken in 1925 by the Russian scholar Kozlov at Noin Ula, a burial ground in Mongolia well to the south of the Siberian town of Irkutsk, revealed the grave of a Hunnish chieftain of the second century B.C. Though the burial was not a frozen one, the soil in which it had been made was so dry that many of the normally perishable objects placed in graves were found there in good condition.

A shaft led to the burial chamber, where the chieftain's body was found lying in a wooden coffin which had been placed on a superb textile—a sort of carpet bearing in appliqué work and embroidery a design showing a griffin, an Altaian type of elk, and a fierce imaginary beast locked in combat amid a setting of flowers and plants. The chieftain's clothes, his personal possessions,

Section of a carpet of Siberian workmanship showing a griffin attacking an elk. From the grave of a Hunnish chieftain buried at Noin Ula, Mongolia, end of the first century B.C.

and the trappings of his horse had all been buried with him. Many of the clothes were of Oriental cut, and among the personal possessions Kozlov found a Chinese ceremonial umbrella and a Chinese lacquer cup bearing an inscription dating from the first century B.C. This Hunnish chieftain must have been an ancestor of those who were later to invade Europe, striking terror wherever they went.

The Sarmatians

At first the Huns who had been dislodged by the Chinese headed toward Ferghana, but later the majority turned westward toward Europe. By doing so, they displaced a tribe known as the Sarmatians, which had been living for centuries on the western fringe of the Asian plain, grazing their cattle north of Lake Ural.

The Sarmatians were an Indo-Iranian people who did not greatly differ either in race or language from the Scythians, though they were not related to them. When first evicted by the Huns they were able to settle in the Caucasus, for the Hunnish pressure, though steady, was at first unhurried. In the course of the third century B.C. they were evicted from the Caucasian lowlands by other invaders, but the ones who had established themselves in the highlands survived there into modern times. They were called the Ossetians, and were among the best-loved of all Caucasian people.

As pressure from the east increased on the lowland

Sarmatians, they began to attack the Scythians living on their western borders, and at each encounter the Sarmatians scored a victory over these experienced warriors. Probably much of the Sarmatians' success was due to their use of the metal stirrup—an invention for which they themselves may well have been responsible. The metal stirrup made it possible for the Sarmatians to use heavy cavalry units in their army—men wearing pointed helms and coats of mail who attacked with heavy spears and lances—as well as light cavalry of the Scythian type, mounted archers trained also to use the sword.

Furthermore, although the Sarmatians followed a patriarchal way of life, they expected their unmarried women to swell the ranks of the army by fighting in it beside their menfolk. Indeed, no Sarmatian girl was allowed to marry until she had killed at least one enemy in battle, and it may well have been the exploits of these hardy young women, who, once married, were to devote themselves wholeheartedly to the care of their homes and families, that furnished the material for the Greek tales about the Amazons. Their help in battle must assuredly have contributed to the Sarmatians' victory over the Scythians.

By the beginning of the Christian era, the Sarmatians had evicted the Scythians from the south Russian plain, forcing them into the Crimea on the one side and into central Europe on the other.

Like the Scythians before them, the Sarmatians established a culture which was followed by a number of related tribes, the Alans and the Roxalans in particular. All these, and foremost among them the Sarmatians themselves, continued to lead much the same sort of life as the Scythians had done, even to the extent of practicing the same kind of animal art. However, they were a less imaginative and, artistically, a less gifted people than the Scythians, with the result that they had to look further afield for their artists and meet some of their needs by means of imports.

Some of their jewelry came from Persia and Mesopotamia as well as from the Greek colonial cities of the Black Sea. Much of it was decorated with geometric patterns or with animal designs of Scythian character, though these are generally less spirited and exciting in appearance than those which the Scythians produced. To make up for this lack, the Sarmatians introduced as much color as possible into their jewelry, arms and horse trappings, producing what are known as polychrome effects in their metal decorations by means of various types of semiprecious stones and enamel inlays in a wide range of colors. Judging by the number of gold vessels and jeweled objects found in their graves, the Sarmatians must have been just as wealthy as the Scythians.

Scythian Neapolis

When the Sarmatians invaded and took control of the grasslands lying west of the Don, many of the Royal Scyths crossed into the Crimea. For a time they remained powerful, continuing to rule over this new kingdom, and providing it with a capital which is now known as Scythian Neapolis. Their might was still sufficient to enable them to become the protectors of Olbia when that flourishing city was reduced to a ruinous condition after a raid carried out on it by a tribe of Asiatic nomads.

The founders of the Scythian domain in the Crimea were their king, Skylurus, and his son Palakus, stone sculptures of whom have been discovered in recent years in the ruins of their capital. In the second half of the first century B.C., Skylurus began to mint his own coins at Neapolis, using both gold and electrum for the purpose.

Scythian Neapolis was defended from attack by stout walls some twenty-five feet high and made of rough stone set in coarse mortar, with defense towers protecting its gateways. The town itself covered an area of some forty acres. Its better houses resembled those of the Greek colonial cities, being built of stone and roofed with tiles; in some of the grander ones there were rooms with mural paintings decorating the walls. But most of the Scythians still preferred to live in tents as their forebears had done, and they continued to bury their dead kings and warriors in magnificent tombs, surrounding them with their best possessions and their favorite horses.

King Palakus cannot have been as wise a ruler as his father, for he became obsessed with the desire to annex Chersonesus. As he advanced to attack this city, its terrified inhabitants appealed for help to Mithridates Eupator (123–63 B.C.), the powerful ruler of the Pontus, a kingdom formed in 148 B.C. which stretched from the southern shores of the Black Sea across northeast Asia Minor, over much of present-day Turkey. Mithridates was a remarkable and fascinating man, as clever a military commander as he was an administrator, wise enough to take the trouble to learn the languages of all the people over whom he ruled. He quickly went to the aid of the besieged townsmen, and inflicted so severe a defeat on the Scythians that they never recovered from it.

After settling matters in the Crimea, Mithridates began to want to conquer the northern shores of the Black Sea, and in order to do so he proceeded to establish military bases at strategic points from which to attack Rome—a power which he detested and which was rapidly gaining control of the civilized world of its day.

Some Roman legions commanded by Pompey had indeed already entered Asia Minor and penetrated northeastward into Armenia. Pompey was now recalled and put in charge of an army which set out across the Balkans to forestall Mithridates by settling garrisons in southern Russia.

The Romans chose Chersonesus as their headquarters. They were able to build a chain of forts along the Crimean peninsula and, feeling themselves secure, they then launched an attack against Mithridates. The fighting which followed was extremely fierce. Mithridates' son deserted to the enemy and, perhaps partly as a result of this, the Romans were able completely to defeat the Pontic army. Bitterly disappointed, Mithridates fled to Panticapaeum where, having tried to commit suicide by drinking poison, which failed to take effect, he ordered a slave to kill him. His body was handed to Pompey who arranged for it to be taken to Sinop so that it might be buried beside those of the earlier Pontic kings.

The Coming of the Goths

The kingdom which Mithridates had established in what is now southern Russia did not end with his death. It continued to be governed by his descendants as vassals of Rome, with Roman temples rising in the market squares of the towns in which the Greek colonials had centuries before them built temples to the predecessors of the Roman gods. However, toward the end of the second century A.D. a number of Teutonic and German tribes, known to us today as the Goths, started moving southward from the mouth of the Vistula where they had been living. Entering the Russian forest belt, they conquered all whom they met. Crossing into the parklands and continuing their advance into the plain, they destroyed the villages and killed the Sarmatians who ruled there.

By the third century A.D. the Goths had become masters of southern Russia. But their power was not to endure, for the Huns suddenly increased the speed of their migration westward and poured into southern Russia, killing the inhabitants and devastating the countryside. Such Goths as could escape death in battle hurriedly invaded western Europe, where they met with so little resistance that, in A.D. 410, they were able to enter and sack Rome.

The Huns did not settle in Russia, however. Early in the fifth century A.D., their chieftain Attila (A.D. 406?–453), who was in the habit of boasting that no grass would grow where his horse had once trod, led them out of devastated Russia into Hungary. His successor, Alaric, proved equally warlike. He too attacked Rome, and was able to impose a huge tribute on the emperors of Rome and Byzantium. But when he invaded Gaul, he was finally defeated by Charlemagne.

Though the Goths and the Huns had been merciless to the Sarmatian and other tribes whom they encountered in southern Russia, they spared the Greek inhabitants of the coastal towns because of their industrial skill. They greatly appreciated the work of the Greek jewelers, especially those of Panticapaeum, and just as these jewelers had formerly worked willingly for the Scythians, learning thereby to produce animal designs of Scythian character, and had continued to furnish the Sarmatians with the jewelry they wanted, so they now showed themselves ready to satisfy their new masters, disregarding their rough manners and cruel ways.

The Goths took a particular pleasure in the Scythian animal style and also the polychrome decorations which the Sarmatians had been so fond of. The Greek jewelers

Cast bronze Scythian standard in the form of a large-beaked bird's head. Note the tiny figure of a stag inserted in a characteristically Scythian manner on the neck.

were skilled in both styles, and provided the Goths with objects in which animals of the Scythian type were prominent, especially large beaked birds. The Goths also demanded geometric patterns combined with polychrome effects.

When the Goths moved to western Europe they thus carried with them many Scythian animal motifs and elements of the polychrome style developed by the Sarmatians. These they introduced among others to Avar tribesmen living in what is now Germany. The Avars took a fancy to some of these designs and began blending them with patterns they had adopted from the Roman world.

In this way, even though the Scythians themselves had died out, something of their art survived in western Europe, where its influence continued to make itself felt until the Middle Ages.

The Pagan Slavs

WHILE THE affairs which were described in the last chapter were taking place in the south, a completely different situation had developed in the north. From quite early times the northernmost sections of western Russia had been inhabited by Finno-Ugrian tribes, who may perhaps have been of Mongolian origin. Not only were they the oldest inhabitants of the area, but also the most primitive.

During the opening centuries of the Christian Era many of them began moving southward into the forest belt, settling in what is today Finland and the Leningrad area of Russia. These Finns had avoided coming into contact with the Scythians, Sarmatians, Goths, and

Huns, and they wished to do the same with regard to their new neighbors.

The more important of their eastern neighbors lived between the Volga and the Urals, in what is now known as the district of Perm, and consisted of some settlers of Slav origin and Turki nomads, and, at a rather later date, of Asiatic Bulgars. Those to their west were Slavs and Lithuanians, living in the area stretching from the Baltic Sea to the river Dnieper. The Finns were a hunting folk, and neither the Slavs nor the Lithuanians showed any desire to interfere with their customs or occupations. The pleasant relationships which were established among these various groups resulted in the Finns gradually beginning to blend with the Slavs.

Very little is known about the Slavs, who were also at this time a primitive people. They practiced polygamy, indulged in blood feuds, and believed in magic and witchcraft, but they were industrious and brave. There were several groups of them. When the Goths were penetrating into southern Russia, a large number of Slavs who had been living in the foothills of the Carpathians began to migrate. Some advanced into what are known today as the Balkans, while others moved westward, to settle in what are now Czechoslovakia and Poland, and others traveled eastward to become the Russians of modern times. By the seventh century A.D. many of these had settled along the Dnieper, around Lake Ilmen, along the Oka, the upper Volga and the western Dvina—the

Bronze fibula in the shape of a woman, with bird terminals, from the seventh century A.D. **(From the Historical Museum, Moscow)**

very regions which had become the homelands of the Finns.

The lives of both the Finns and the Slavs living in these areas were controlled by the geographical character of the land. Its chief features were its rivers, both large and small, forming a veritable network across it. These rivers were rich in fish, and they provided an easy and quick means of communication between one group of settlers and another, since most of them lived along the riverbanks in clearings made from the dense forests of the region.

The majority of the settlers chose to live on one of the great waterways which linked the Baltic either to the Caspian Sea and the Asiatic people beyond, or led to the Black Sea and the vast and mighty Byzantine Empire which stretched over much of Asia and Europe. Trappers and traders were able to earn quite a good living by sending their furs and goods to distant lands by either of these routes, but for the agriculturists who lived some distance away from these waterways, life was both hard and dangerous.

When the Goths had been evicted from the southern part of the country by the Huns, and the Huns had themselves turned their backs on all but the most westerly section of the plain, the rest of it had been left open to yet another wave of Asiatic raiders. These new invaders were of Mongol origin, and in the sixth century A.D. a group of them known as Avars penetrated to the coast of the Black Sea and gained control over much of the hinterland, even overflowing into the Hungarian plain. There they remained until some time in the eighth century A.D., when they were in their turn overrun and destroyed by some allied Germanic and Slav tribes. But before these Slavs were able to install themselves in what had been Avar territory, another Mongolian tribe, that of the Ugrians, advanced from central Asia.

The Khazars

Like the Huns before them, the Ugrians did not remain in Russia but pushed on into central Europe to become the Hungarians of our day. As they advanced westward the Ugrians were followed into Russia by another tribe, that of the Khazars, and this group liked it so well in Russia that they decided to remain in the southeastern part of the country. The Khazars must have been both numerous and efficient, for they appear to have had little difficulty in founding a kingdom which endured until the tenth century A.D., and which stretched, when at its most powerful and prosperous, from the Caucasian mountains to the Dnieper on one side, and across the Volga on the other.

To begin with, the Khazars ruled over the local Slavs, but as the years passed they found it increasingly difficult to prevent central Asian tribesmen of Turco-Tartar blood from crossing into southern Russia in a constant series of fierce and devastating raids. These tribesmen included the Petchenegs, a Turkish people, whose descendants continue to the present day to live as nomads in the remoter districts of northern Persia, and the Polovtsians, whose spirited dances form such an exciting interlude in Borodin's opera *Prince Igor.* But these raiders rarely entered the forest zone, the density and darkness of which terrified them after the vast, open expanses of the Eurasian plain to which they were accustomed.

Nevertheless, the Slavs living in clearings along the

Cast silver amulet of a horse from the pagan Slav burial at Malinovka, near Kiev, sixth century A.D.

riverbanks remained in constant terror of these tribesmen, and whenever rumors of a nomadic raid reached them they at once abandoned their villages, even though these were protected by a vallum, or earth wall. Taking their valuables with them, they would hurry into the forest, often in their fear burying their treasures beneath a tree, at times never to find them again. It is only with the disappearance of some forest land in modern times and the cultivation of the cleared areas that some of these buried hoards have been recovered from their hiding-places.

The Khazars became a seminomadic people content to

live in town during the winter months but, like many a Turk of later times, anxious to spend the summers in the country, tending their vines, fishing their great rivers, and selling their goods at a profit to any purchaser who might turn up.

The trade routes connecting Europe to Asia ran through their land, and gradually trading centers grew up, such as the citadel of Satchel on the Don, the town of Itil on the lower Volga, and that of Semeden in the Caucasus. Similar centers were also created on the central reaches of the Volga by the eastern Bulgars, a people who had succeeded in establishing themselves in that area in the eighth century B.C., where they spent their days harassing their Finnish neighbors and expanding their foreign trade.

To all these towns came merchants, whether pagan, Jewish, Christian, or Mohammedan. The Jews were in a majority, and their influence was so great that they eventually persuaded the Khazar rulers to adopt Judaism, though the bulk of the Khazar people remained either pagans or Moslems while a few became Christians.

The Slavs began coming to these important trading centers as early as the eighth century A.D., and possibly even earlier, and an idea of the volume of the business which they transacted can be gained from considering the great number of superb Byzantine silver dishes and other objects of value which entered Russia between the fourth and the end of the seventh centuries A.D., and are now to be seen in many of the country's leading museums. Then, in the eighth century A.D., Arabian merchants, following in the steps of the Arab soldiers who had conquered Persia, overrun the Caucasus and penetrated into central Asia, also appeared in these markets, and their dealings with the Slavs account for the vast hoards of Arabian coins dating from the eighth to the tenth century A.D. which have been discovered in various parts of Russia in modern times.

The Slavs were not satisfied in establishing commercial relations only with their eastern and southern neighbors. They gradually began to turn their attention to the northwest where, separated from them by only a narrow strip of water, lived the Varangian or Swedish people in what is known today as Scandinavia. In the ninth century, at the very time that the Norwegian Vikings were raiding England, the Slavs began to employ some of the Swedes—who had probably come to their land to trade—as mercenaries in the garrisons they were forming to protect their more important towns from the fierce raiding parties of covetous Petchenegs and Polovtsians.

Some of these Nordic mercenaries stayed on in the Slav towns after their contracts expired and set themselves up as merchants, for they had quickly realized that great profits could be derived from trading with Byzantium. Soon the volume of goods traveling by river to the Black Sea and onward to Constantinople became so great that the route was spoken of as "the road leading from the Varangians to the Greeks." Towns such as

Novgorod, Polotsk, Smolensk, Lubech, Chernigov, and Kiev, to name but a few, grew to a considerable size, and in them the patriarchal way of life began to give way to a community rule. An increasing number of Varangians settled in them, intermarrying and mixing with the Slavs —without, however, leaving any deep or lasting mark on their art or culture.

The more important a town became, the stronger the garrison it needed. The Varangians had proved splendid fighters and their services were, therefore, always welcomed in the defense force organized by each town. The ablest of these mercenaries often succeeded in becoming, first, officers, then commanders, whose powers sometimes came to equal that of the local Slav princes and chieftains. Among the first Varangians to establish themselves in positions of complete authority were Askold and Dire, co-rulers of Kiev, in the mid-ninth century, and Rurik, ruler of Novgorod, who was to become the founder of Russia's first reigning house. Some of his descendants are still living today.

Askold and Dire must have had a very strong army at their command, for in A.D. 860 they ventured to go to war with Byzantium—the strongest empire of the time. Their daring was not groundless, for they emerged from the contest unvanquished and with their reputation enhanced. However, their achievement brought no results with it, and Kiev's real period of greatness did not begin until twenty years later. It followed upon Rurik's death in Novgorod in 879 when Oleg (to give him the Russianized form of the Norse name of Helgi), as guardian of Rurik's young son Igor (or Ingvarr in Scandinavian), assumed control of Novgorodian affairs and set about enlarging the young chieftain's domain.

The Early Rulers of Kiev

Annexing Smolensk and Lubech, Oleg won Kiev by a trick and put Askold and Dire to death. He found Kiev so attractive a city that he decided to settle there rather than in Novgorod; and in order that the other princes in the land should realize that he intended to become their ruler, he proclaimed Kiev his capital and the mother of all Slav towns. Kiev thus became the kernel of the country which was soon to become known to the world as Rus, the medieval term for Russia.

Oleg did not live long enough to unite the Russian principalities under Kiev's authority. Indeed, much of his time had to be spent in strengthening his frontiers. He began by establishing a chain of fortified towns along his northern boundary. Next he set out to destroy the power of the Khazars. When he had succeeded in this, he built a network of forts along his eastern frontiers so as to protect the agriculturists living in the open country from raiding nomads.

He completed these tasks by A.D. 907, and he then assembled a mighty army and a large number of boats which he arranged to have mounted on wheels so that they could be transported overland from one waterway to another with ease and speed. When all was ready he led his forces against Byzantium, commanding his men with such skill that he was able to besiege Constantinople and eventually to force the Greeks to open peace negotiations.

Oleg's death occurred in a strange manner. Like most of his contemporaries, he was a superstitious man, so that when a fortuneteller told him that his favorite charger would cause his death, Oleg sadly gave orders for the horse to be put to grass and never used again. Many years later, Oleg was standing on a hillock when he noticed a horse's skull lying at his feet. He was told that it was the skeleton of his once-loved charger. Bitterly distressed, Oleg approached the heap of bones, upbraiding the fortuneteller for his error. So concerned was he that he failed to notice a poisonous snake creep out of the dead animal's skull. It attacked Oleg without warning, and he died as a result of its bite.

Igor followed Oleg as ruler of Kiev. He was a far less able man than Oleg, and although he tried to pursue Oleg's policy of uniting the princes under his authority and led two campaigns against Byzantium, he achieved little success in either direction. He met his death ingloriously, being murdered with his small bodyguard when bent on obtaining a second, unowed, payment of tribute money from one of the tribes subjected to him. Although the cause of his death was dishonorable, he and his men died bravely.

His widow Olga took control of Kievian affairs after

Igor's death. She proved a wise and efficient ruler. The first task which she set herself was to establish peaceful relations with Byzantium. Accordingly, in A.D. 957, she set out on a state visit to Constantinople, the most renowned capital of its time, a city famed for its magnificent churches and fabulous palaces. Its splendor and beauty exceeded even Olga's expectations. She was deeply impressed by its magnificence. The Byzantine emperor thought it expedient to accord her the honors due to a queen, and Olga was greatly stirred and gratified by her reception.

But she was even more deeply affected by her first contacts there with Christianity. Its creed won her heart, and the beauty of the services held in the great cathedral of St. Sophia made so strong an impression upon her that she decided to become a Christian. She was accordingly baptized in St. Sophia, still today perhaps the world's finest cathedral, in a ceremony of great pomp jointly conducted by the Byzantine emperor and the Patriarch, the head of the Greek Orthodox Church.

On Olga's return to Kiev, her son Sviatoslav, though the first member of the ruling Kievian house to bear a Slav instead of a Norse name, refused to follow her example. He was a typical Varangian, preferring soldiering to all else, and he remained a confirmed pagan to his death. He was succeeded on the throne by his younger son Vladimir who ruled from 980 to 1015.

Vladimir had to deal with many important military and constitutional problems throughout his life, but the most far-reaching of his decisions concerned the religion of his people. He had himself become a Christian quite early in his life, choosing to join the Greek Orthodox Church of Byzantium in preference to the Catholic Church of Rome. His preference was probably dictated by his desire to marry a princess of the Byzantine royal house, but legend relates that before making up his mind as to which branch of Christianity to adopt he sent ambassadors to examine the religious observances of his neighbors.

When the envoys he had sent to Byzantium returned saying that on entering the great cathedral of St. Sophia at Constantinople they thought that they had been to heaven, his choice was made. In A.D. 988 Vladimir's subjects were given mass baptism.

This step brought Kievian Russia into the Christian world of its day, but the choice of the Greek Orthodox in preference to the Roman Catholic ritual linked Russia with Byzantium instead of with the Western world, thus affecting the whole future of her political outlook.

Kiev and Novgorod

THE PAGAN Slavs worshiped various gods whom they represented by tall, rough-looking carvings shaped something like a totem pole, which they erected in their market squares and public places. Christianity made it necessary for these idols to be replaced by churches.

The Russian towns of the pagan period undoubtedly contained some impressive buildings amid the humbler cottages, but even these were built of wood, which was the local building material. The Greek ability to build in stone had been forgotten even by the coastal inhabitants during the grim years of the Gothic and Hunnish invasions. Some Russians had become converted to Christianity in the days of Askold and Dire, and a tiny church had been built in Kiev in Igor's day, but it could not have been more than a wooden chapel, and it may well have been built by Greeks.

When Vladimir found it necessary to provide his people with churches, church furnishings, and priests, no Russians could meet his needs, and he was obliged to turn to Byzantium—from which he had acquired his chosen form of Christianity—and probably also to the Greeks of Byzantine Chersonesus, now called Korsun by the Russians. It was from these places that the architects, masons, and artists whom Vladimir needed came, as well as some of the clergy. In this way the Russian Church became from the very start an offshoot of the Greek Orthodox Church of Constantinople, and the architectural and artistic styles which the early Russians took over were those that had been fully developed in the Byzantine world.

The Byzantines were a highly cultivated people, who for centuries had helped to produce and had delighted in an extremely complicated and very advanced culture, while the newly converted Russians had only recently stepped out of a condition bordering on barbarism. The Russians were, nevertheless, able from the start to understand the foreign art which was being introduced to them, and to appreciate its beauty. They quickly came to love it, and having done so they were able within a very short time to master its techniques.

At first the Russian builders and artists began by work-

The Cathedral of St. Sophia, Novgorod, 1045-52. Already the Byzantine dome has begun evolving into the Russian, onion-shaped one.

ing beside the visiting Greeks in the capacity of pupils, but they were quickly promoted to becoming their assistants, and before very much longer some of them began working independently. The churches which were first built in Russia followed Byzantine lines, retaining a cruciform plan, with three or five aisles and the domed roofs of the Greek models—features which remain characteristic of all Greek Orthodox Church architecture to this day, whether practiced in Greece, Russia, Bulgaria, Yugoslavia, or Slovakia. The introduction of these buildings into Kievian Russia altered the face of the land by the new outlines which they introduced, while the arts necessary for adorning the interiors of these churches opened the door to the magic world of visual creativeness, a world which entranced the Russians.

Innumerable churches sprang up throughout Russia within a very short time after the country's conversion. Some were no more than tiny wooden chapels; others, like the great thirteen-domed wooden cathedral of St. Sophia of Novgorod, were impressive structures of brick or wood. Novgorod's St. Sophia was destroyed by fire, to be replaced in 1052 by the superb stone building which still survives. The finest churches were those built in stone under the guidance of Greek architects. When Dittmar, Bishop of Megibur, visited Kiev in the year 1018 he was astonished to count four hundred churches standing within the walls of what was then a very small town.

The most magnificent of all Kiev's churches had not by then even been begun—the great Cathedral of St. Sophia, named after the world-renowned church built in the sixth century in Constantinople by the Emperor Justinian. The foundation stone of Kiev's St. Sophia was laid by the Grand Duke of Kiev, Yaroslav the Wise, in 1037; and within another thirty years the magnificent mosaics and paintings in its interior had been completed. The finished work is of the greatest beauty, one able to hold its own today beside the finest cathedrals of western Europe of a similar date.

The wall paintings and mosaics in the body of Kiev's St. Sophia are concerned with telling the story of the

Scriptures, but one group displays the portraits of Yaroslav the Wise and his family, while the walls of the staircase to the Grand Duke's private pew are decorated with scenes from the games which were held in the hippodrome at Constantinople on festive occasions. They are unique in their choice of subject, and the only pictorial record to survive of the entertainments which delighted alike the court circles and the humblest inhabitants of Constantinople in the years of its great glory.

In the Orthodox world religious paintings are known as *icons*; the majority are painted on panels and are used in the church services in much the same way as the religious pictures produced by the Primitive painters of Italy were used in Roman Catholic churches. One of Kiev's treasures was an icon of the Virgin and Child which was specially commissioned in Constantinople by a Kievian prince in about 1125. It reached the Russian capital well before the middle of the same century, but was later moved to various other cities. Known today as the *Virgin of Vladimir*, it is to be numbered with the world's greatest religious paintings.

Christianity not only introduced to the Russians a new form of religion; it brought with it literacy, and the ability to read led to a new understanding of charity, kindliness, and righteousness. "Ignorance is darkness, learning is light" is a saying which expressed the general opinion of the people, and it is one which continues to prevail in the U.S.S.R. today. The alphabet used by the Russians was one which two scholars called Cyril and

Two wall paintings from the Cathedral of St. Sophia, Kiev. ABOVE: *a portrait of the four daughters of Grand Duke Yaroslav, painted about 1045.* BELOW: *a musician from the series of frescoes depicting the games held in the Hippodrome at Constantinople.*

The icon of the Virgin of Vladimir.

Methodius had produced for the use of the Slavonic-speaking people of Bulgaria; it is called Cyrillic after its inventor Cyril. With his assistant Methodius, Cyril ranks as a saint of the Greek Orthodox Church.

Schools run by priests were established throughout Russia, often as part of a monastery. Scholars, many of them priests, were produced in them; and the pursuit of knowledge helped to arouse in the educated an interest in history which, in its turn, served to develop a sense of nationality among the diverse groups of people forming Kievian Russia. In 1074 Nestor, a monk of Kiev's great Monastery of the Caves, began to take note of all that he was able to discover about the past, from the creation of the world down to the happenings of his own day. He entered all he learned into what has become Russia's first chronicle. Early in the twelfth century Sylvester, a monk of Kiev's Vidubetsky monastery, brought the chronicle down to his own time, and from then onward historians, many of them living in such important towns as Novgorod, Pskov, or Suzdal, produced similar records.

The ability to read also made it possible for the Russians to make use of Byzantine books on law, administration, land tenure, and agriculture. Literature in the form of biblical tales, lives of saints, epics, and *byliny,* or heroic poems, also came into being. The earliest and loveliest of the epics, *The Lay of Igor's Campaign,* dates from about 1185. It commemorates the bravery in battle of the grandson of Oleg, Prince Igor, when campaigning against the Polovtsian nomads. It tells how Igor put his foot in his golden stirrup to mount his horse and led his men into battle for his country's sake. As he neared the Don, "the birds in the oak trees lay in wait for his misfortune; the wolves stirred up a storm in the ravines; the eagles by their screeching called the beasts to [a feast of] bones; the foxes yelped at the scarlet shields. O land of Russia, you are already beyond the hill." (I. Obolensky, *The Penguin Book of Russian Verse.*)

Under the grand duke Yaroslav the Wise (1015–54), the young country's future seemed rich in promise. Learning and the arts had taken a firm hold on its productive soil, and Christian standards of conduct and uprightness as understood by the Byzantines of the period had begun to regulate people's behavior. Indeed the country was beginning to play a part in European affairs. Yaroslav's marriage to the Swedish princess Ingigerd—who, on coming to Russia, assumed the Slavonic name of Irene—made it easier for him to send ambassadors to Germany, Hungary, Poland, Scandinavia, and even as far away as France. As a result, he was able to marry three sons to the daughters of German princes, and a fourth to a Byzantine princess, and also to give one daughter in marriage to the king of France, another to the king of Hungary, and a third to the king of Norway.

Commercial relations between these countries and Russia resulted from these unions, but Yaroslav devoted most of his own leisure to codifying and amending existing laws in the light of the Christian outlook, so that at his death he left his people with a sound legal system.

Yet for all his wisdom Yaroslav proved an overindulgent father; he could not bring himself to bequeath the whole of his grand duchy to only one of his sons. Instead, he divided it into principalities which he distributed among them, though leaving Kiev, and with it the powers of supreme authority and the rank of grand duke, to his eldest son.

At his death this arrangement led to jealousy among his sons, and their quarrels lasted for a good many years. The author of *The Lay of Igor's Campaign* tells that Kiev "groaned with sorrow, and Chernigov with affliction. Anguish flowed over the land of Russia, sorrow in abundance spread across the Russian land. And the princes forged strife each against the other, while the infidels, victoriously invading the land of Russia, took tribute of a squirrel-skin from every homestead."

Novgorod tired of the situation and broke away, to set itself up under its own prince as a republican city-state. The poor throughout Russia suffered acutely from the unrest. Many were reduced to such dire poverty that, abandoning their homes, they fled eastward with their families to settle on the Don and Dnieper, where they formed the Cossack communities of later times. Others fled to the Oka and the Volga, areas which were sparsely inhabited by a few Finns. Settling for preference along the river edges, they gradually intermarried with the Finns, forming the group of people known today as the Great Russians, to distinguish them ethnically from the Little or Small Russians of the Kievian region.

Some of the emigrants soon became prosperous, and towns such as Suzdal and Rostov sprang up and attracted so many inhabitants that by the latter half of the twelfth century the district in which they were situated was thriving. The Grand Duke of Kiev decided to establish his youngest son Uri, nicknamed Dolgoruki or "Long-armed," as prince of the area. On leaving Kiev, Uri took with him the icon of the Virgin of Vladimir, and when his son set up his capital at Vladimir he began building a cathedral for his city which could serve also as a shrine for the icon. Thus, this particular painting has always been known as *The Virgin of Vladimir.*

Under the reign of Uri, as well as under those of his son and nephew, the city of Vladimir competed with Kiev as Russia's capital, but Vladimir was only one of the many new towns which the three rulers established. Moscow, which had until then been no more than an insignificant village, received its first mention in a chronicle in 1147.

Cathedrals and Icons

During the century covered by the reigns of these three princes, from 1100–1216, the artistic achievements of what had become known as the Vladimir-Suzdalian principality became particularly remarkable. Exquisitely proportioned churches built of sparkling Kama sandstone rose in considerable numbers, often in settings of great natural beauty. For the first time in the history of Russian architecture their exteriors were adorned with

LEFT: *the Cathedral of St. Dimitri, Vladimir, late twelfth century. Built of Kama sandstone, it is elaborately decorated with low relief sculptures of biblical, floral, and animal forms.* RIGHT: *detail of a window in the Cathedral of St. Dimitri.*

numerous sculptures. Not all of these were of a religious character. Many consisted of floral or animal designs, but although none had any real connection with its neighbor, all were so cleverly and harmoniously placed that they produced very pleasing and decorative effects.

In style these sculptures are quite different from anything that had as yet been seen in Russia. Today some people try to account for their unusual appearance by ascribing them to the influence of artists from western Europe, while others attribute them to the principality's links with the Caucasus which led to the marriage of Uri's grandson with the Georgian queen Tamara.

It is, however, not without interest to note that some of the animals which appear in these sculptures bear quite a clear resemblance to the beasts which figure in Scythian art. This suggests that the Russian peasants may have continued throughout the centuries to decorate their own possessions with some of the designs which had survived from Scythian times.

The interiors of Russia's churches were covered with mural paintings illustrating the Scriptures. The scenes shown were the same as those which the earliest Christians had depicted on the walls of the first churches to have been built in the Byzantine Empire, and which the later Byzantines had continued to present unaltered in the churches which they built and decorated. Throughout the centuries, the Byzantines had firmly avoided any change either in the appearance of these scenes or even in their location, in order that anyone entering a church situated in any part of the empire would know exactly where to find his favorite scene and would be able to recognize it instantly.

In addition to the wall paintings, it had been the custom in Byzantium to place small versions of the biblical scenes and the figures of holy or saintly personages in various other parts of the churches, particularly on altar screens. The early Christians painted these small versions of the mural scenes on wooden panels that had been coated on one side with a layer of gesso, which provided much the same sort of surface as the layer of plaster on a wall. They were known as icons.

The Cathedral of St. George at Yuriev-Polski, 1230-34. The façade of the church is decorated with many fine sculptures.

Sculptures in the Cathedral of St. George at Yuriev-Polski. On the left, a column and capital decorated with designs of classical inspiration. On the right, two saints portrayed in the native style which the Russians evolved from the Byzantine.

Late fifteenth century Novgorodian icon of St. Florus and St. Laurus, the twin brothers who are the patron saints of grooms and horses. They appear above standing on either side of St. Michael, who holds the reins of their horses, and they are seen again below, riding with their brother Seth to guard a herd of horses.

When the gesso had hardened it was polished until it became absolutely smooth. The artist then generally drew the outline of his picture in cinnabar, a form of bright red paint. After this he painted the background, but instead of giving the scene a blue sky, he painted a gold one because gold, being a precious material, was the most fitting of all colors for representing the glories of heaven. Russians also quite often used silver, and eventually even came to prefer white, red, or even green backgrounds.

When the background had dried, the artist turned his attention to his chosen scene, using tempera paint diluted in yolk of egg. Most of the artists were monks, and there seems to have been some degree of specializing, for some painted only the faces, while others painted the figures and others filled in the detail. Some of the finest artists, however, preferred to do the entire work themselves.

Many of Russia's earlier icons were imported from Byzantium. The icon of the Virgin of Vladimir was one of these, and a number of other examples of very high artistic quality survive, though many more perished in wars or the fires which occurred frequently in the wooden towns of medieval Russia. A considerable number of icons by Russian artists also exist, the earliest dating from the twelfth and thirteenth centuries. Icons of this date are extremely rare, and those that have survived are numbered among Russia's chief treasures.

The Russians of medieval times seem on the whole to

have been fonder of icons than of wall paintings, and the number of icons which were placed in their churches became so great that it led to the invention, sometime in the course of the fourteenth century, of a sort of altar screen known as an *iconostasis*, or "stand for icons."

This structure was erected between the body of the church and the sanctuary, stretching across the whole width of the building. It was made of wood, carved and painted and covered with gold leaf in the richer churches. Icons were placed on it according to a carefully prescribed order. Even modest iconostases contained three rows, or tiers as they are generally called, while larger ones had as many as five. All had at their center a low, double door, known as the Royal Door, decorated with paintings and opening on to the altar. A single door was set at either side of the iconostasis to open into the side apses of the church.

While the principality of Vladimir-Suzdal prospered and the cultural life of much of the rest of Russia was fast developing, quarrels broke out anew among the princes over the vexed question of supreme authority. Kiev's military strength was greatly diminished as a result of them, and her army was further weakened by the desertion of men who preferred to serve one or other of the princes rather than the Grand Duke. This loss in efficiency occurred at a disastrous moment, for just when events were dividing Russians at home, Asia entered upon another period of unrest.

The Mongol Invasion

This time the Mongols and Tartars were on the move. Led by Genghis Khan, a cruel and formidable commander, they started to advance westward. On reaching the Caucasus some of them turned to invade Persia, spreading terror and misery wherever they went. They eventually captured Baghdad and overran much of western Turkey. Other groups headed toward Russia. In an effort to halt them, the princes patched up their quarrels, assembled what forces they could, and marched eastward to resist the enemy.

The two armies met in battle on the banks of the river Kalka in the Dnieper country in the year 1223. It quickly became evident that the hurriedly assembled and insufficiently trained Russian troops were no match for the all-conquering Asiatics. The Russians were forced to retreat and were pursued almost to the walls of Kiev. The Asiatics plundered the towns and villages they overran, killing or kidnaping the inhabitants. Then, with Kiev in sight, the invaders suddenly withdrew.

But in 1237 they reappeared, led by Batai, as fierce and formidable a commander as Genghis Khan had been before him. This time the Mongols seized Ryazan, and captured and devastated lovely Vladimir, though its famous icon was spared. As they advanced deep into Russian territory, the princes again hurriedly mustered their men and once more set out in a vain attempt to stop the advance. On this occasion the armies met in battle close to the river Sit, and again the Russians were completely defeated.

After subjugating Kiev, looting its treasures, and destroying many of its finest churches, the Mongols then turned toward Novgorod. Fortunately winter was at hand, and in that harsh climate its approach put an end to further fighting, at any rate for the time being. The Novgorodians took advantage of the lull to prepare themselves for the spring offensive.

When fighting resumed, the Mongols had lost interest. By the end of the summer, though they established a firm hold over the whole of eastern and central Russia, Novgorod was saved. Leaving only a small occupying force and some senior officials in control of the key towns, the bulk of the Mongols withdrew to the Volga, where they founded the Kingdom of the Golden Horde, with its capital at Saray on the lower Volga.

From there they dominated the conquered regions of Russia. They forced the Russian princes, whom they permitted to govern their hereditary lands, to act as their representatives, levying the large sums of money which had to be paid to the Mongols each year from every Russian household.

The Mongol occupation of Russia was to last for over two hundred years, until A.D. 1480, and for the first hundred and forty years life in the occupied districts could do no more than mark time. Schools were closed, cultural and artistic activities were at a standstill. Russia was never to make good the loss that this represented to her intellectual growth. The inhabitants in the occupied areas had to direct all their efforts first at ensuring their survival by meeting their daily needs, then to doing everything within their power to preserve unfaded and unaltered the religious, cultural, and artistic traditions which had been developed by their parents and grandparents between the time of Russia's conversion to Christianity and the Mongol invasion of their country. Only in Novgorod, which was never occupied, was life able to flow along normal lines, but even this was achieved under the threat of another war.

Alexander Nevsky

This time the danger came from the west, where covetous German and Lithuanian commanders, seeking to draw advantage from the disorganization resulting from the Mongol invasion, attempted to capture Novgorod and gain control of her territory. The peril became so acute that the republican, self-governing Novgorodians hastened to appeal to their hereditary prince, whose name was Alexander, to take command of their troops and confront the enemy.

Alexander was a very remarkable man; his bravery was outstanding and he proved himself to be a notable military commander. Supported by the stalwart Novgorodian soldiery, he gave battle to the enemy on the banks of the river Neva. The magnificent story of his stand, which ended in the complete defeat of the German enemy, is the subject of a thrilling film which was made some thirty years ago by the Soviet film producer Eisenstein, and which is now universally recognized as a classic. It is called *Alexander Nevsky,* meaning Alexander of the Neva, for the Novgorodians unanimously awarded this title to their heroic commander in honor of his victory. As impressive as the victory itself, though less widely appreciated, was the skill with which Alexander used the advantage it gave him in the diplomatic talks which he held afterward with the Mongol Khan of the Golden Horde in Saray. At these parleys Alexander ensured the independence of his Novgorodians in exchange for an annual payment of ready money.

The security which Alexander won for his Novgorodians left them free to consider their future. They had always depended upon foreign trade for much of their wealth, and they now applied themselves to renewing their commercial contacts with the outer world. The Mongol occupation of Kiev and much of southern Russia had had the effect of reducing and slowing up Novgorod's trade with Byzantium, so the Novgorodians now turned to western Europe to fill the gap.

By a sustained effort they succeeded fairly quickly in establishing a flourishing trade with their Baltic and German neighbors. In addition to wealth, this trade brought them many intellectual advantages, for it kept them in touch with western Europe where a more liberal and advanced way of life had been evolved, and it enabled them to develop their talents in a way which was impossible to the Russians living in the occupied zone.

An artist can do his best only when he feels himself to be completely free, and when the people who surround him are able to share his interests and outlook, thereby providing the stimulating atmosphere which is necessary to a creative artist. Such an atmosphere of freedom prevailed only in Novgorod, and thus the future of Russian art and culture came to rest in Novgorodian hands. As a result, there dawned in Novgorod what is now regarded as the classical period in the history of Russian medieval art.

Public meeting in medieval Novgorod; painting by the nineteenth century Russian artist, A. P. Ryabushkin.

By this time medieval Novgorod had grown into a handsome town. Its streets were paved with oak planks, and were pleasanter and easier to walk along than those of many a western town of equal importance. The town was divided into two sections by the river Volkhov which runs through it. The western part contained the kremlin, or citadel, the cathedral of St. Sophia, and the prince's palace. In the eastern section was the square in which the Novgorodians assembled to decide by a majority vote on all matters of national importance.

The house of a rich merchant at Pskov, near Novgorod, which, though built in the eighteenth century, follows a much earlier architectural model.

Most of the houses in both parts of the town were two-storied buildings constructed of wood. The lower floors were used as storerooms, while the upper contained the owner's living quarters. The standard of living was a high one, and practically the entire population could read and write—although in the schools and also for all forms of public and private business, birch bark was used to write on instead of paper.

Accustomed as they were to handling goods of the finest quality coming from various parts of Europe and Asia, the Novgorodians developed a keen appreciation of beauty and quality. The tastes they had formed dictated the art and architecture which grew up at this period within Novgorodian lands. It expressed itself first and foremost in the tall and severe proportions of their churches, which took on an entirely different appearance from that of the churches erected in Byzantium or in western Europe. The domes with which the churches were roofed also acquired a new look, for the lower Byzantine outline was discarded in favor of the essentially Russian onion-shaped form.

By the side of these churches the Novgorodians raised elegant free-standing bell towers, the inspiration for which may well have come to them from Italy, though the shapes were entirely novel and basically Russian. They fitted numerous bells into these towers and their chimes could be heard far afield, penetrating the winter stillness and summer's heat haze, bringing messages of hope and encouragement to many people.

Two examples of the Novgorodian style of church architecture. **LEFT:** *A photograph of the Monastery Church of St. George, built in 1119.* **RIGHT:** *A drawing of the west front of the Church of the Saviour, built in 1198-99.*

BELOW, LEFT: *A later example of Novgorodian architecture—the Cathedral of the Trinity, Pskov, 1365-67.* **RIGHT:** *A humble wooden church from the village of Panilovo. Though dating from the sixteenth century, it follows a far earlier model, and shows definite influences of the Novgorod style.*

Painting kept pace with architecture. The interiors of the new churches became covered with superb frescoes and their iconostases were filled with icons of astonishing beauty. In all their works the artists continued to present the biblical scenes in exactly the same way as they had always been shown.

In icon painting, even though no two icons are ever completely identical, the outward form of a given subject always remains much the same, so that even someone who cannot read will instantly recognize the scene which is represented. Nor does the meaning underlying the scene change as it does with every painting of our own day. It is the intensity of this meaning, the degree of faith which inspired the artist, his sense and use of color, his feeling for line, which distinguish a good icon from a less accomplished one.

A young monk called Andrei Rublev, working between 1380 and 1420, produced some of the most beautiful, most delicate and flowing, vivid yet harmoniously colored of all Russian icons. They rank with Russia's greatest artistic achievements, yet Rublev was not the only outstanding religious artist of his day. There were many others who also created superb paintings which occupy places of honor in Russia's museums. However, the names of the men who painted these pictures remain unknown, for, like Rublev and the artists of Byzantium, none of the earlier painters of the Greek Orthodox Church signed their works because they believed in producing them for the glory of God rather than for their own fame.

Icon of the Old Testament Trinity painted in about 1411 by Andrei Rublev.

Rublev never signed his paintings, either. His name, together with those of two or three others, has been saved from forgetfulness only because some contemporary chronicler, filled with intense admiration for his work, felt moved to mention the name in connection with some supremely successful paintings. One such entry in a chronicle refers to the lovely icon of the Old Testament Trinity which Andrei Rublev painted in about the year 1411 in honor of Cyril of Radonezh, abbot of the Monastery of the Trinity at Zagorsk, near Moscow, in which Rublev was a monk. It is a painting of supreme beauty.

The Rise of Moscow

In a country in which the quarrels of the princes had destroyed all sense of national unity, it never occurred to the Novgorodians, so well satisfied were they with the conditions and culture they had created for themselves, to spare much thought for the wider political issues.

Yet in the fourteenth century the general situation in Russia was of a thoroughly depressing character. Most of the princes, though figureheads in their own lands, were little more than puppets of the Mongols who remained firmly established on the banks of the Volga. Nor were the Mongols the only invaders of Kievian Russia; the whole of the Crimea was likewise occupied by dangerous and restless Nogay and Crimean Tartar tribes, while

Russia's northwestern frontiers were constantly being threatened by neighboring Poles, Lithuanians, and Germans.

Fortunately the tiny principality of Moscow was in good hands. At Alexander Nevsky's death it had fallen to his youngest son, Prince Daniel, who left it to his son Ivan. At the time, the town of Moscow was still so tiny that it occupied no more than a third of the present-day Kremlin enclosure and boasted only two churches. The majority of the houses were mere cottages which clustered around the only slightly larger wooden house built on the highest point to serve as the prince's palace. All these houses were equipped with a stove, for efficient heating is essential in Moscow's climate; but in many of the houses the smoke still escaped from a hole in the roof, and only the better ones were provided with chimneys. The town was fortified against invasion by stout wooden walls. On one side of it, the river Moscow provided additional protection, while the river Neglinnaya did so on another.

Ivan Kalita

Prince Ivan was never crowned, but he is now generally described as Ivan I. He ruled his principality from 1328 to 1341, and was soon nicknamed by his people Kalita, meaning "Moneybag," or "the Gatherer." The name was an apt one, for Ivan was the first Russian to

Laying the first walls of the Moscow Kremlin in 1156; painting by the nineteenth century Russian artist, A. M. Vasnetsov.

realize that his country's future as a great power depended upon its ability to regain its political independence. He realized too that the only way in which this could be achieved was by the union of all the principalities into one nation.

Finding that he could not persuade any of the princes to recognize him as supreme ruler, Ivan set about buying up the poorer ones, and since many of them had been reduced to a condition of extreme poverty, the sight of ready money quickly decided them to sell out. After enlarging his territory by means of a number of quite small purchases, Ivan was able to increase his capital quite considerably, and he used the money he was able to save to buy out more important princes. At last his principality became so large that it was able to compete in importance with such units as self-governing Novgorod, Ryazan, Rostov, and Yaroslavl.

Ivan's greater wealth also made it possible for him to give the Khan of the Golden Horde better presents than the other princes could, and since there is a good deal of truth in the French remark that "gifts help to keep a friendship alive," Ivan won the affection of Russia's Mongol overlord. As a result, the Khan appointed Ivan collector of taxes throughout the whole of occupied Russia, and also raised him to the position of Grand Duke—supreme prince throughout the land.

Ivan's head was not turned by these honors, and he never forgot his plan to unify Russia as a first step toward regaining her freedom. Nor did he forget the miseries which had resulted in Kievian Russia from the arrangement by which supreme authority over the princes passed, not to the dead Grand Duke's son, but to the senior male member of his family. To avoid a repetition of similar difficulties, Ivan arranged for the title to pass for ever onward from father to son, in the manner which was customary both in Byzantium and in western Europe. This law, together with some other wise measures, brought peace and wealth to his subjects.

Conditions in Moscow became so much better than anywhere else in the land, with the possible exception of Novgorod, that many people were tempted to settle in Moscow. Eventually even the Metropolitan, as the head of the Russian Church was called, decided to move from Vladimir to Moscow. His presence there automatically conferred upon Moscow the character of a capital city, though at first it was in fact no more than the chief town in a large principality.

Dimitri

Ivan's son continued his father's policy of unification, though he did so with less energy and ability. In 1359 he was succeeded by his son Dimitri, who showed throughout his life much of the energy and ability which had distinguished his grandfather, Ivan Kalita. In addition Dimitri was also a military commander of genius. His first success was the annexation of the powerful principality of Tver.

Moscow had by then spread out far beyond the original Kremlin walls, and whole districts now lay outside the walls, unprotected from the enemy. Dimitri determined to remedy this by building new walls round the larger city. Instead of building them of oak as had been customary, he set about constructing them of stone. After they were completed he felt justified in testing the strength of his Mongol overlords. When the next payment of Russia's tribute money fell due, Dimitri refused to hand it over. His behavior enraged the Khan of the Golden Horde, who lost no time in mustering his men. Not content with this, he sent envoys to the Lithuanians to persuade the latter to attack Russia from the northwest, and so to start a war on two fronts. News of this move reached Dimitri as he neared the Don at the head of his army.

Anxious to deal with his enemies singly, he decided to attack the Mongols without delay. On the morning of September 8, 1380, having first commended their souls to God, the Russians crossed the Don, screened from the enemy by a heavy mist. An early morning breeze soon blew away the haze to reveal a vast Tartar force mustered in brilliant sunshine on the field of Kulikovo. As the sun broke through, the figure of a huge horseman detached itself from the enemy's ranks and rode toward the Russians to issue a fiery challenge. A young monk riding near Dimitri instantly spurred his horse forward and galloped to answer the call. He had been a gallant soldier in the days before he had taken his vows. When his spear met that of the Tartar challenger, the force of the impact was so great that both riders were thrown off their horses, and fell dead on the ground.

Then the trumpets of both armies sounded the attack and the battle began. It raged all day, extending over an area of some seven miles. The bitter fighting brought advantages first to one side then to the other, but eventually the horsemen of the Golden Horde managed to make a gap in the Russian lines. Convinced that the victory was theirs, the entire Mongol force poured

The Battle of Kulikovo; painting by A. M. Vasnetsov.

through the opening. Dimitri had been holding some of his men back for just such an eventuality, and he now led them into the fray.

Striking the Mongols in the rear, Dimitri's troops were able to change the course of the battle and to secure a decisive victory for Russia. It was not itself sufficient to end the Mongol hold on the country, but it was enough to unnerve the invaders and to convince the Russians that the complete overthrow of their enemy was no longer a mere dream, but a definite possibility.

In spite of their heavy casualties, the victory put such heart into the Russians that the creative spirit which had lain dormant in them for so long stirred again. The arts and letters began to revive, and the wave of optimism which swept through the country is clearly reflected in the serene happiness of Rublev's paintings, for Rublev was quite a young man at the time of the battle of Kulikovo. As a result, all of Rublev's works belong to the period when the Russians had begun to realize that their liberation was in sight. Dimitri became the country's hero, and the people expressed their admiration and gratitude by calling him Dimitri Donskoi, meaning "of the Don," in honor of his achievement. He well deserved the title, for it was the victory of Kulikovo which started the transformation of what had been the Grand Duchy of Moscow into what was soon to become the Muscovite kingdom.

After their victory at Kulikovo the Russians never again paid the Mongols tribute money until the latter compelled them to hand it over. To obtain it, the Mongols were often obliged to send troops into Muscovy. On several occasions these expeditions were on such a large scale that the invaders were able to besiege Moscow, and on one or two occasions even to break into it, sacking and destroying parts of the town. Nevertheless, each raid gradually became less serious than the one before it, and it was obvious that the Mongol hold on the country was beginning to weaken. However, it was Tamerlane, and not the Russians themselves, who was eventually to break its grip.

Tamerlane

Tamerlane was the ruthless chieftain of a Tartar tribe, the Berlas, whose capital was at Samarkand in Central Asia. He attacked the Kingdom of the Golden Horde twice, first in 1390 and then four years later. On the second occasion it became obvious that this dreaded man, who was probably responsible for more widespread misery than any other figure in history except Hitler of Nazi Germany, was planning to invade Russian-controlled territory.

By this time Basil I had succeeded his father Dimitri Donskoi as Grand Duke of Muscovy. Appalled at the prospect of entering into a war with Tamerlane, he nevertheless mustered his army and rallied the princes to his aid. He felt, however, that he desperately needed God's aid during the coming ordeal, so he sent to Vladimir asking for the loan of the city's miraculous Byzantine icon of the Virgin of Vladimir. He hoped that the prayers directed to the Virgin in heaven might with the icon's participation result in obtaining divine protection for his country. Only after the request had been sent did Basil set out with his army to face Tamerlane.

But on the very day on which the icon reached Moscow and was set up in the Cathedral of the Assumption, within the Kremlin walls, suddenly and for no apparent reason Tamerlane started withdrawing from Russian territory, and Basil was able to return to Moscow without having had to give battle. The entire population of

Tamerlane. From an old German engraving.

Moscow ascribed the miracle to the icon, and would not agree to allow its return to Vladimir. The icon, therefore, stayed permanently in Moscow, remaining in the Cathedral of the Assumption until the outbreak of the Revolution in 1917, when it was moved to the Tretiakov Gallery in Moscow. There it continues to draw large crowds of visitors. But a copy of the icon was commissioned from the leading Russian artist of the day, none other than Andrei Rublev, and it was despatched to Vladimir to replace the original icon.

Whatever the regret that the inhabitants of that town

may at first have felt at the loss of their original icon, Rublev's substitute painting was of such high quality that they soon ceased to retain any ill feelings about the matter.

Both Ivan Kalita and Dimitri of the Don had been so much engaged in the business of unifying northeastern Russia that they had been unable to spare any attention for the situation which had arisen on their southwestern border. Lithuania had taken advantage of this to try to seize the Kievian territory which is known today as the Ukraine, meaning the border country.

The Lithuanians of the period were still pagans, and as they penetrated into Kiev's former possessions they started to adopt some of the customs and beliefs with which they came in contact there. Notwithstanding the lowering of standards which had resulted from the Mongol occupation, Kiev remained more cultured than Lithuania. Some Lithuanians even acquired a smattering of Russian.

But this Russianization of the Lithuanians did not last long. The sudden death of the king of Poland had left that country without a ruler, and the Lithuanian chieftain took advantage of the situation to propose marriage to the daughter of the dead king. Since she was a Roman Catholic, the Lithuanian ruler had to become one in order to marry her. The marriage united Poland and Lithuania, and the new sovereign accepted the culture, outlook, and political views of the far more cultured Poles. Poland was a traditional enemy of Russia, and when, somewhat later, Poland and Lithuania split into two kingdoms again, the Lithuanians retained the anti-Russian feelings which they had acquired from the Poles. It was then that they annexed Smolensk and determined to seize Kiev, thereby arousing the anger not only of Basil I and his subjects, who were powerless to deal effectively with them, but also of countless generations of Russians to come.

Moscow, the "Third Rome"

In 1453 the Turks succeeded in capturing Constantinople, thereby putting an end to the existence of the once all-powerful Byzantine Empire. In southeastern Europe the news was regarded as disastrous. The collapse of Byzantium left Russia as the only Orthodox country in a position to govern itself. Many Greeks, for the word Byzantine is used to describe the Greeks living anywhere in the vast Byzantine Empire from the third to the fifteenth century A.D., fled for safety from the Turks to Italy and Russia.

The last Byzantine emperor had died gallantly fighting on the ramparts to defend his capital against the Turks, but other members of his family had escaped the general massacre which followed Constantinople's fall. Some of these had settled in Italy as refugees, among them a young princess of the royal house, Sophia Palaeologos. At the death of the wife of Ivan III, ruler of Moscow at this time, the Pope conceived the idea of

Left: ***The Royal Arms of Muscovite Russia.*** **Right:** ***The Royal Cap of Monomachus.***

effecting a marriage between the widowed Grand Duke and the young princess.

The idea appealed to Ivan, and a Russian embassy set out for Rome to settle the matter and to bring Sophia back to Russia. She reached Moscow on November 12, 1472 and was married to Ivan on the same day. She brought with her the Byzantine royal arms, consisting of the double-headed eagle; it was added to the mounted figure of St. George used by the Grand Dukes of Moscow as their crest, and from then onward the combined form was used as the arms of imperial Russia until the outbreak of the Revolution in 1917.

Largely as a result of this marriage, Moscow began to be regarded by Orthodox Christians as the third Rome, the successor of Constantinople, which had often been called the "Second Rome," and Ivan III began to think of himself less as a Grand Duke than as a royal sovereign. Even though he had not been crowned, he began calling himself Czar—the Russian rendering of the Latin word Caesar—when receiving foreign guests. On such occasions he often appeared wearing royal robes and the Cap of Monomachus, which is Russia's equivalent of a coronation crown.

The First Czar

In domestic affairs the most important task which Ivan III had to settle concerned the future of Novgorod, which still remained independent. Fearing Muscovite domination, certain Novgorodians had secretly begun negotiations of a political character with the Lithuanians, and this made the union of Novgorod and Moscow even more imperative. After failing to persuade Novgorod to merge voluntarily with Moscow, Ivan laid siege to the town. When it eventually capitulated, he tried both to break Novgorodian might and also to reconcile the people to the loss of their independence, and to persuade some of the town's leading icon painters to move their workshops to the capital. The Novgorodians who did so found conditions in Moscow congenial. As a result, other artists came to Moscow of their own accord. The icons painted in Moscow at the time belong to what is known as the transitional period of Muscovite painting.

Ivan was anxious to beautify Moscow and—perhaps encouraged by his wife, who had been educated in Florence when that city was teeming with the artists and intellectuals responsible for the Italian Renaissance—he sent to Italy for architects. At the same time he instructed his ambassadors to persuade foreign artists to seek employment in Moscow and also to purchase foreign works of art. Those foreigners who accepted his invitations were given many privileges and rewards. But the unfortunate fact that no Western power had come to the aid of Christian Russia when that country found herself attacked by the Mongols had had the effect of making Russians distrust their Western neighbors, even though they were Christians, fully as much as they mistrusted their Moslem and pagan ones.

This distrust developed into deep suspicion at the sight of foreigners, whose different customs and whose habit of portraying holy personages naturalistically in their art shocked the Russians, who were accustomed to the severe Byzantine traditions. Because of this, the foreigners who came to Moscow were all obliged to live in a particular quarter of the town, which came to be known as the German village, for the word "German" was applied by the Russians to all Westerners. In this way contacts between West-Europeans and Russians were of the slightest.

Nevertheless, the artists of both groups met on many

A present-day view of the Moscow Kremlin showing the brick walls dating from the end of the fifteenth century, the bell tower of Ivan III, the Kremlin cathedrals, and, on the extreme left, one of the palaces.

occasions, and those who were employed in the royal workshops situated in the Palace of Arms within the Kremlin did so regularly. As a result, Russian silversmiths and also Russian painters began to get to know something about artistic trends abroad, and many of the painters began to feel dissatisfied with the strict laws imposed upon them by their Church. They wished especially to experiment in naturalistic painting and portraiture, new developments which the Church viewed

The Palace of Facets in the Moscow Kremlin. In the background can be seen the domes of the three churches of the Redeemer.

with suspicion and which it forbade its artists to follow. Because of this ban the Western style in art continued to remain virtually unknown in Russia.

The impact made by the Italian architects whom Ivan III imported to Moscow was greater than that of the foreign artists employed in the Palace of Arms workshops, but it was not as profound as might have been expected. Though these architects were responsible for building the walls of the Kremlin—they designed those which still exist today—as well as for rebuilding the Cathedral of the Assumption and also a new royal palace, the finished buildings were far more Russian in appearance than they were Italian. This is even true of the palace, which was called the Palace of Facets, because the surface of the stones of which it was built was cut into facets in the way which was popular at the time in Bologna. This is to be explained by the influence exercised on artists by their surroundings, which was so deeply felt that it even altered the character of men's work while they lived in Russia. The same happened time and again throughout the eighteenth century. In the Moscow of the fifteenth and sixteenth centuries it was the order of the day. Not only the Italian architects, but artists working in the Palace of Arms, regardless of whether they came from western Europe, Persia, or Byzantium, acquired Russian characteristics, which are clearly reflected in their work.

The Czars of Muscovy

WHEN IVAN III died in 1505 he left to his son Basil a free and strong kingdom which had nothing to fear from its eastern neighbors, nor from the Tartars living in the Crimea, though it was still necessary to be wary of Poland and Lithuania and to guard against possible German attacks. It was also essential for Muscovy to extend her contacts with western Europe if she was to regain the regard which the Western world had formerly begun to feel for Kievian Rus.

Basil's son Ivan IV was only three years old at the time of his father's death in 1533. His mother could not prevent control of affairs from falling into the hands of a group of noblemen who cared less about Russia's prosperity and their grand duke's welfare than their own interests. Indeed, they treated the young prince so harshly that his character became marked for life, and in his later years he often fell into a condition bordering on insanity, during which he committed acts of such appalling cruelty that, notwithstanding his numerous and often quite remarkable achievements, he is known to history as Ivan the Terrible.

Ivan the Terrible

By the time he was sixteen Ivan could endure no longer the misrule and insults of his nobles. With great courage and determination he informed them that he intended to assume full control of his country. He insisted on being crowned Czar, thus becoming the first Russian ruler to reign as an anointed king.

Ivan was by far the cleverest ruler of the House of Kalita, and for all his cruelty he proved himself to be an outstandingly able administrator. In the military field he took the offensive against the Tartars who were living on his eastern boundaries, and in 1552 conquered their stronghold of Kazan. The victory was largely due to Ivan's gunners, who were the first Russian troops ever to carry firearms. Even so, the siege of the fortress of Kazan lasted for several months. When it at last fell, the victory was celebrated throughout Russia.

In Moscow the church dedicated to St. Basil the Beatified, which still stands in Red Square, was built to commemorate the victory. The work was entrusted to

Ivan the Terrible.

two Russian architects called Postnik and Barma, who devised a plan consisting of a main central church with seven chapels grouped around it, each of which was dedicated to the saint on whose day the Russians had won a notable victory. Later, the number of these chapels was increased to eight, all of which were connected by passages and roofed by a many-colored, onion-shaped dome.

The conquest of Kazan was followed seven years later by that of Astrakhan. Then in 1582, toward the end of Ivan's life, Siberia—Russia's first Asiatic conquest—was added to his realm. Its annexation was not achieved by the Czar's army but as a result of a private venture undertaken by one of the families of great merchant princes, the Stroganovs, which had sprung up in Russia under Ivan III.

The Stroganov estates were situated in the district of Perm, which lies, roughly speaking, between the Volga and the Urals, in an area rich in salt and mineral deposits. Their land was being constantly raided by wild

Red Square in Moscow during the reign of Ivan the Terrible. At the left can be seen St. Basil's Cathedral under construction. Painting by A. M. Vasnetsov.

tribesmen, the subjects of Kuchuma, ruler of much of western Siberia. To protect themselves and their people, the Stroganovs had been obliged to form a strong defensive force, and when five hundred tough Cossacks with their chieftain Ermak at their head appeared to join the Stroganov garrison, the family decided that the time had come to punish Kuchuma's men. The eight hundred fighters were equipped with firearms, and it was this advantage, coupled with Ermak's skill as a military leader, which transformed what had been intended as a purely private punitive expedition into a conquest of national importance.

Ivan the Terrible was not only interested in warfare; he also showed concern for intellectual matters, and it was he who introduced the printing press to Moscow. Though the town scribes, fearing to find themselves out of work, broke up the first press, they were unable to prevent others being set up in its place.

The introduction of the printed book had many important results. It led to a revived interest in Russia's earlier history, and it also helped to make educated Russians realize how out of touch they were with the artistic and cultural advances which had taken place in western Europe.

Thus, although most Russians still continued to regard the West with suspicion and dislike, and to cling more firmly than ever to their own often outdated customs, a group of people grew up in Moscow who wished to see their country developing along more advanced lines and catching up with western Europe's achievements, not only in the fields of art and letters but also in the scientific ones.

Ivan himself did not share these views, having acquired his ideas of a sovereign's rights and powers, and borrowed his system of taxation, from the Mongols. But he did recognize the need for establishing regular contacts with the leading powers of western Europe. His wars against Lithuania and Poland, though fought mainly to safeguard his frontiers, were also aimed at gaining a northern outlet to the sea—a far-seeing ambition which Peter the Great was to realize a century and a quarter later, thereby completing Russia's reinstatement as an influential power.

Ivan the Terrible had to content himself with sending embassies abroad, and it was in his day that the first English reached Russia. Their appearance there was due to chance, for they had set out from the Thames in three ships in order to seek a northern sea route to China. Two of their ships foundered in the Arctic Sea, but the one commanded by Captain Richard Chancellor managed to reach the Northern Dvina River. The local Russians could make nothing of the new arrivals, and sent Chancellor to Moscow. He was so well received at court there that, on returning to England, he set about persuading Queen Elizabeth to enter into diplomatic and commercial relations with Russia.

Two years later Chancellor was back in Moscow as the Queen's official representative. This time he was re-

A silver and niello loving cup made in Moscow for Czar Fedor.

ceived with even greater pomp than on his first visit, and his dispatches home are full of amazement at the splendor of the Russian court. At one of the functions which he attended he was surprised to find that over two hundred guests were all "serve in gold vessells," and that, on another occasion, the plate on display there included "four marvellous great pottes or crudences as they call them of gold and silver. I think they were a good yarde and a half hie." He was equally impressed by the jewels, magnificent furs, and fabulous horse-trappings belonging to the courtiers, but he was considerably shocked by the amount of make-up used by the women.

Ivan's son and successor Fedor I was an excessively mild and weak man. His interests were wholly centered on Church affairs, and it was he who raised the head of the Russian Church from the status of a Metropolitan to that of Patriarch, the latter title having until then been reserved for the chief dignitaries of the Byzantine Church. Fedor left the government of his realm to his brother-in-law, Boris Godunov, and when Fedor died childless, it was Boris who eventually succeeded him on the Muscovite throne.

At first Boris ruled wisely and well, but later he became obsessed by the desire that his son, who was also called Fedor after the late Czar, should succeed him on the throne—an ambition which led Boris to neglect affairs of state, and which also served to rouse the jealousy of many nobles, who thought that they had an equal right to the throne. The tragic events of Boris Godunov's closing years form the subject of a stirring opera, the music for which was composed by Moussorgsky.

Boris' son did eventually succeed his father, but at a time when he was far too young and inexperienced to govern. His incompetence led to civil war, and Poland took advantage of the upheaval to attempt to put a usurper on the throne, and through him, to gain control of Russia. At this the whole country rose to Moscow's defense. In a fierce battle fought on the walls and in the very outskirts of the city, the Poles were driven back. Russia's independence was once again secured, but her throne still remained vacant because no male member of the House of Kalita remained alive to fill it.

The political crisis was eventually resolved in February, 1613, when representatives drawn from all over Russia elected a young nobleman called Michael Romanov to become their Czar. Though Michael was only sixteen, the choice fell on him partly because he was personally popular, partly because he was related to Ivan the Terrible's first wife, and partly too because his father, the Metropolitan Filaret, was a prisoner-of-war in Poland.

The skill with which this very young man dealt with the numerous problems confronting him as Czar of Muscovy is often apt to pass unnoticed, perhaps as a result of the modesty with which he set about solving them. After the years of unrest and fighting he found his Treasury empty, his country poverty-stricken and the prey of highwaymen, thieves, and all manner of thugs. Worse still, it was again being threatened by the Poles and the Swedes, attacking on different fronts. While trying to prevent any serious breakthrough of either enemy, Michael was obliged to work out a new system of taxation and to apply it to his people. As a result, funds gradually began to flow back into the Treasury's coffers, but not before the Swedes had managed to capture Novgorod, though they were finally halted at Pskov.

The money enabled Michael to assemble a considerable army. When the Swedes learned that it was ready to go into action, they showed themselves willing to discuss peace terms. By these terms Novgorod was restored

Czar Michael Romanov.

to Russia, but the Swedes retained the whole of the coastal area of the Gulf of Finland. Having secured peace in the north, Michael turned his attention to the Poles, who were advancing to besiege Moscow. After fierce fighting and heavy casualties on both sides, Michael was able to secure a truce of fourteen and a half years and an exchange of prisoners. Among the Russians returned was the Czar's father, Filaret; Michael lost no time in elevating him to the office of Patriarch and assigning to him the duties of a co-ruler.

Life at Michael's court was very similar to that led in any average Russian household of the day. Like everyone else in the country, the Czar, his family, and his courtiers rose at about four every morning and spent several hours at prayer before attending to the day's business. At ten all went to church. Dinner followed at midday, after which practically the entire population went to bed, rising only when the church bells summoned them to evensong. The rest of the evening was again devoted to business, and the day ended with supper followed by prayers. When all had retired to rest, the night watchmen appeared in the streets, breaking the silence at regular intervals with their patrol cries.

Like other Orientals, the Mongols who had occupied Russia kept their women in seclusion. The Russians had also adopted this habit, though they did not carry it to the same lengths as the Mongols had done. Thus, Russian women never wore the Oriental veil, nor were they forbidden to appear before strange men, nor were they excluded from parts of their houses, though they were expected to spend most of their time in the women's quarters and to be seen in the rest of the house only when invited to do so. A married woman had to obtain her husband's permission whenever she wanted to leave the house to visit friends, and unmarried girls could do so only to attend church.

All women had to throw a scarf over their faces whenever they went out. But holidays were spent gaily by both men and women. Although much of every day had to be devoted to prayer, much of it was also spent watching wrestling matches, admiring the antics of dancing bears and performing dogs, and attending performances given by professional dancers, musicians, actors, and mummers. In wintertime tobogganing was popular, and chess and draughts were favorite indoor games. The Church often disapproved of these entertainments but it was powerless to stop them, nor could it curb the passion for hunting and feasting, which was shared by rich and poor alike. When friends came to a house they were received by their host's wife, who welcomed them warmly before sitting them down to an immense meal.

It was under Michael and his son Alexis I (1645–76) that the people of Russia really came to love Moscow as well as to admire her, regarding her both as the heart and also the capital of their country. They realized that it was Moscow which had united the various Russian principalities into a nation, that the relics of many venerated saints were now assembled there, and that the city had become the successor to Constantinople in so far as the Orthodox Church was concerned. It was in Moscow that the Czar and the Patriarch resided—the two champions of the Orthodox Christians living under Moslem rule in the Ottoman Empire.

Life in Seventeenth Century Moscow

Once again people began to flock to Moscow, and the town grew considerably larger, spreading out over the neighboring hills into the forests beyond. A white stone outer defense wall had been built to protect the new districts, and from the heart of the town rose the tall tower of Ivan the Great. This also was built in white stone so that Russians began to refer to their capital as "the white-walled, golden-spired" city. Yet, apart from the outer walls, the bell tower, Ivan III's Palace of Facets, and many of the churches, the bulk of the city remained a wooden town, in the middle of which rose the red brick walls and towers of the Kremlin.

The bridges spanning the rivers were all built of wood. Regardless of constant appeals from the authorities, who were anxious to reduce the danger of fire, people continued to live in wooden houses because they considered them healthier. Even when the Czar appealed to those who could afford it to build in stone, people would do little more than construct the ground floors, which they used as storerooms, in stone, persisting in using wood for the construction of the upper story, in which their living quarters were situated. In these the floors were covered with carpets and the walls with hangings, though in the all-too-rare stone houses mural decorations were popular. The women's and children's quarters were often situated in the high attics, many of which were provided with attractive, overhanging balconies.

Richer houses also possessed an external section known as a klet, or cell, in which the wooden walls were not plastered, and the rooms were used as bedrooms during the hot summer months. The royal palace at

A late seventeenth century print showing a procession leading into the wooden palace of Kolomenskoe, near Moscow, built in the course of the sixteenth century by the czars of the Kalita dynasty.

Kolomenskoe and the stately home of the Stroganovs in the district of Perm were architectural marvels, with their varied roof lines and sprawling yet captivating façades.

The Muscovites were so profoundly religious that although many of them were quite content to live in small wooden houses, they were anxious to build splendid stone and wooden churches and chapels to the greater glory of God. They were also extremely fond of decorative effects. In their homes they surrounded themselves with painted furniture, beautifully embroidered linens and silks, and splendidly worked gold, silver, and enamel vessels. In their churches they expressed themselves in sculpture, carvings, and paint. Windows and doors were set within large stone frames carved with lacelike decorations, and the drums of the domes and the cornices set along the tops of the walls were adorned with sculptured patterns such as dogtooth molding. The churches were roofed with tiers of splendid gables whose curious shapes corresponded to those of the women's headdresses, the *kokoshniks*. Over these were raised domes of onion shape, topped with slender crosses whose delicate outlines cut a tracery in the sky. Sometimes the dome was replaced with an equally picturesque tent-shaped tower.

Inside, they covered the walls with superb religious paintings, and set up vast, elaborately carved, gilt and painted iconostases holding icons whose clear-cut lines and intense colors instantly drew the eye. Adding the final touches of splendor were church vessels skillfully fashioned in silver and gold, and often decorated with jewels and enamels, admirably proportioned metal candlesticks and superb embroideries, many of them adorned with seed pearls.

The fuller, more diverse way of life evolving in Moscow represented a great step forward, even though it failed to catch up with the advances made by western Europe during the centuries when Russia was stagnating under the Mongols. But it also led to the rise of a strongly marked class society. In it the Czar and the

Carved window frame for a village house dating from the seventeenth or eighteenth century. Note the design motifs inherited from Scythian times.

Two seventeenth century copper candlesticks of Muscovite workmanship.

Embroidered chasuble from the seventeenth century.

A sixteenth century boyar.

Church held pride of place. Next came the nobles and courtiers, or *boyars* as they were called, who formed a highly privileged group owning vast country estates. The gentry were less fortunate. Although they were expected to present themselves fully armed, mounted, and equipped to defend their country when called upon to do so, they were provided in return with land held on a system of life tenure only. However, it was the peasants who were by far the least lucky. They owned no land, though they worked it on behalf of the boyars and the gentry. They were expected to pay taxes just as the merchants and town dwellers had to do, and they also had to pay a rent to their masters for their small holdings and to set aside certain days of the week on which to cultivate their masters' lands free of charge.

At first the peasants had been free to move on St. George's Day of each year from one landlord to another. But the departure of several families of peasants from a village caused difficulties for those who remained, since the tax assessment was levied on a village as a whole and not on the individual householders. Those who stayed on in a village had to make good the sums due by those who had left it, so a peasant's departure was disapproved of as much by his fellow peasants as by his landlord, who was often obliged, even when needed by his regiment, to stay on his farm to deal with the labor difficulties which had arisen.

A landlord's absence from his regiment endangered the state, and aroused the concern and disapproval of the government. To solve the difficulty, it became the custom to tie a peasant to a particular landlord and a specific village by writing his name in a book. The new measure deprived the peasant of his right of free movement and reduced him to a state of serfdom.

The evils which resulted from this cruel act are incalculable, and their ill effect still continues to make itself felt. A peasant tied to a bad landlord could only hope to improve his condition by escaping. The number who succeeded in doing so under Ivan the Terrible was so great that many fields throughout the country remained untilled, and Ivan's son, the devout but hard-hearted Fedor, found himself obliged to agree to a law making it necessary for any man caught within five years of his escape to be returned to his original owner. Michael, the first Romanov, extended the period to fifteen years. However, the landlords were not satisfied by this and demanded that the period should be extended to life. In the early 1700's Peter the Great, though so enlightened in some respects, agreed to this monstrous wish; and in the very century in which a period of so-called Enlightenment dawned in western Europe, the peasants of Russia were reduced to a condition of complete slavery. The vile practice was only abolished in 1861, when Czar Alexander II insisted on their freedom being restored to the peasants.

The civil war which raged in Russia after the death of Boris Godunov's son Fedor, and the attacks launched against the country by Poland and Sweden, had the effect of again hindering Russia's intercourse with western Europe. Alexis, the second Romanov, was made keenly aware of this when, in his loneliness following the death of his first wife, he began visiting the house of the boyar Matveev, one of his closest friends. Matveev had married a Scots girl and his house was run on European lines; these greatly impressed the Czar. So, too, did a young kinswoman of Matveev who lived in his house, where she had been brought up on Western lines. In due course the Czar married the young girl, and in 1672 a son was born to them. The boy was called Peter. He was the Czar's seventeenth child, but his third surviving son, and his two stepbrothers were extremely delicate. Peter was an exceptionally healthy baby, and his father adored him. Alexis died, however, when Peter was only four years old, long before anyone could tell that the child would go down in history as the Czar Peter the Great of Russia.

Peter the Great

Peter was the only child of royal birth to receive an excellent education. At the age of five he was given a tutor who taught him to read, write, and count, but Peter had so great a thirst for knowledge that he soon outstripped his master. One day Prince Dolgoruki gave Peter an astrolabe which he had bought for him abroad. An astrolabe is a compact instrument for observing the positions of the celestial bodies, but neither the boy nor his tutor, nor for that matter anyone else in the royal circle, knew how to use it. Peter was determined to find out how to do so. At the first opportunity he asked the German court doctor to explain the instrument to him, but the doctor was no better informed than the rest. However, he introduced Peter to a Dutchman called Timmerman living in the German village in Moscow, and the latter was at last able to enlighten the prince. After that Peter took to haunting Timmerman's house, insisting on being introduced to foreigners of distinction, plying everyone with questions, learning all he could.

When he realized how backward Russia was, he determined to do everything in his power to transform his country into a modern state, to bring its army up to date, to give it a navy and to found schools, technical colleges and universities in which scholars and technicians could be trained. This was a magnificent ambition for a boy of sixteen. To accomplish it, Peter soon after set out for western Europe, where he often traveled under an assumed name and even worked as a shipwright in Holland and England.

On his return to Moscow, Peter at first gave no indication of impending changes. But in 1703, as we have seen in the first chapter, Peter decided to abandon Moscow and to build a new town on the banks of the Neva River near the Gulf of Finland, a strip of land which his army had only recently succeeded in winning from the Swedes. Assured of an outlet to the sea, St. Petersburg, as it was called, was to be Russia's new capital, and serve as the country's "window on to Europe," as Peter himself termed it.

At the same time Czar Peter introduced wide-sweeping reforms, some of which affected the appearance of the people by forcing them to adopt European dress and shave their beards as a first step to becoming integrated into western Europe. To begin with, Peter's laws met with violent opposition, but as St. Petersburg grew to become one of the loveliest cities in Europe, educated Russians came to welcome the changes.

When Peter died in 1725 the transformation he had dreamed of and tirelessly worked for had been accomplished. Russian art, thought, and much of the country's way of life had been firmly established on a new road—one which turned completely away from the past, with its belief in isolationism, and enabled Russia to become a European power of world-wide importance.

It also led to the great Russian cultural achievements of the eighteenth century and pointed the way toward progress for the succeeding periods in Russia's long and vital history.

Index